Spare Us Some Carcasses

And Stop Eating Our Share

An Appeal From The Vultures

By
Dr. Sahadeva dasa

B.com., FCA., AICWA., PhD
Chartered Accountant

Soul Science University Press

Readers interested in the subject matter of this
book are invited to correspond with the publisher at:
SoulScienceUniversity@gmail.com   +91 98490 95990
or visit DrDasa.com

First Edition: February 2014

Soul Science University Press expresses its gratitude to the
Bhaktivedanta Book Trust International (BBT), for the use of quotes by
His Divine Grace A.C.Bhaktivedanta Swami Prabhupada.

©Soul Science University Press
All rights reserved

ISBN 978-93-82947-06-6

Published by:
Dr. Sahadeva dasa for Soul Science University Press

Printed by:
Rainbow Print Pack, Hyderabad

To order a copy write to purnabramhadasa@gmail.com
or buy online: Amazon.com, rlbdeshop.com

Dedicated to....

His Divine Grace A.C.Bhaktivedanta Swami Prabhupada

People have become vultures. And their civilization is a vulture civilization. Animal-eaters -- they're like jackals, vultures, dogs. Flesh is not proper food for human beings. Here in the Vedic culture is civilized food, human food: milk, fruit, vegetables, nuts, grains. Let them learn it.
~ *Prabhupada* (Journey of Self Discovery 6.5: Slaughterhouse Civilization)

By The Same Author

Oil-Final Countdown To A Global Crisis And Its Solutions

End of Modern Civilization And Alternative Future

To Kill Cow Means To End Human Civilization

Cow And Humanity - Made For Each Other

Cows Are Cool - Love 'Em!

Let's Be Friends - A Curious, Calm Cow

Wondrous Glories of Vraja

We Feel Just Like You Do

Tsunami Of Diseases Headed Our Way - Know Your Food Before Time Runs Out

Cow Killing And Beef Export - The Master Plan To Turn India Into A Desert

By 2050

Capitalism Communism And Cowism - A New Economics For The 21st Century

Noble Cow - Munching Grass, Looking Curious And Just Hanging Around

World - Through The Eyes Of Scriptures

To Save Time Is To Lengthen Life

Life Is Nothing But Time - Time Is Life, Life Is Time

An Inch of Time Can Not Be Bought With A Mile of Gold

Lost Time Is Never Found Again

Cow Dung - A Down-To- Earth Solution To Global Warming And Climate

Change

Cow Dung For Food Security And Survival of Human Race

(More information on availability on DrDasa.com)

Contents

Preface

1 Web Of Life And The Future Of Human Race   11

2 Vultures - Nature's Perfect Cleaning Crew   13

3 Vulture - An Introduction   17

4 Vultures - Vanishing In Thin Air   23

5 Lack Of Proper Studies   33

6 Ecosystem service   35

7 Scavenging Birds And Ecosystem Services

    Experience from Germany   40

8 Vultures In Tradition And Culture   42

9 Lack Of Food

    The Most Important And Neglected Reason   45

10 Diclofenac - A Hype And An Alibi   52

11 Vulture Deaths

    Reasons Other Than Dietary Insufficiencies   57

12 Extinction Of Vultures

    Impact And Consequences   64

13 The Bad Press

    And A Thankless Task   70

14 Vultures - No Substitute   74

15 Vulture Restaurants   79

16 Vulture Restaurants In India
   India Throws Vultures A Bone - Literally   82

17 Vulture Restaurants
   Cambodian Experience   85

18 Nepal
   Eateries For Endangered Birds   87

19 South Africa
   New Vulture Restaurants   91

20 South Carolina
   Restaurant For Birds Of Prey   95

21 Spain
   Vulture Restaurants   96

22 Armenia
   Vulture Restaurants - Serving and Saving Vultures   99

23 Human Beings
   The Wingless Vultures   101

24 The Wingless
   Watching The Winged Ones   104

25 International Vulture Awareness Day
   Let's Abstain From Meat For A Day   108

26 A Vulture Civilization   110

27 Say No To Eating Meat
   Humans Are Not Physically Created To Eat Meat   114

28 Food For Vultures
   An Appeal To Restaurants   126

29 Eating
   Civilized And Bestial   130

The Author

Preface

A majority of the world's biologists are convinced that a "mass extinction" of plants and animals is underway that poses a major threat to humans in the next century. Yet most of us are only dimly aware of the problem.

The rapid disappearance of species is ranked as one of the planet's gravest environmental worries, surpassing pollution, global warming and the thinning of the ozone layer, according to the survey of 400 scientists commissioned by New York's American Museum of Natural History.

The poll's release comes on the heels of a groundbreaking study of plant diversity that concluded than at least one in eight known plant species is threatened with extinction. Although scientists are divided over the specific numbers, many believe that the rate of loss is greater now than at any time in history.

"The speed at which species are being lost is much faster than any we've seen in the past -- including extinctions related to meteor collisions," says Daniel Simberloff, a University of Tennessee ecologist and prominent expert in biological diversity who participated in the museum's survey.

Most of his peers apparently agree. Nearly seven out of 10 of the biologists polled say they believe a "mass extinction" is underway, and an equal number predict that up to one-fifth of all living species could disappear within 30 years.

Nearly all attribute the losses to human activity, especially the destruction of plant and animal habitats and poisoning of our planet.

Even the head of the United Nations new biodiversity body, Zakri Abdul Hamid concurs, "The accelerating loss of biodiversity poses a "fundamental threat" to the survival of humankind" as he also sounds the alarm on the declining biodiversity on farms.

Among non-scientists, meanwhile, the subject appears to have made relatively little impression. Sixty percent of the laymen polled professed little or no familiarity with the concept of biological diversity, and barely half ranked species loss as a "major threat."

This is all true, despite the dissenters questioning the validity of these claims. It is evidenced by near extinction of vultures in many countries. In just last two decades, vulture population in India has crashed from 80 million to 8 thousand. Frantic efforts are on to save the remaining few.

Extinction of vultures might be the last straw that would break our planet's back. Vultures are highly specialized to rapidly dispose of large carcasses, thus playing a critical role in nutrient cycling, leading other scavengers to carcasses and reducing the risk of contamination by pathogens by quickly consuming decomposing carcasses.

No other species is as efficient or well equipped to clean our atmosphere and keep us safe.

These vultures are dying because we have encroached upon their food supply. We can survive in myriad of ways but vultures can only survive on one thing - decomposing carcasses.

It's time we seriously think of sparing some carcasses to these poor cousins of ours.

Sahadeva dasa

Dr. Sahadeva dasa
1st March 2014
Secunderabad, India

1.

Web Of Life

And The Future Of Human Race

Human race does not exist in isolation but it's a minuscule link in a complex web of life. Human survival depends on the survival of life on this planet. The delicate web of life can not be disturbed without endangering the human survival itself.

There are millions of species and trillions and quadrillions of other life forms. Fate of all these creatures is intimately connected with that of humanity. Its arrogance and ignorance to think that we can survive in isolation. We, like all other life forms, are products of our environment.

Destroying our environment is like cutting off the branch we sit on. Our present lifestyle is anti-life. Our direct and indirect destruction of life has reached mammoth proportions. In the name of food, we kill over 60 billion animals and birds every year and in the name of economic development, we destroy forests and other species. In fact, It is estimated that a minimum of 54,000 species are becoming extinct each year, about 6 an hour.

Even though the majority of mankind is happily entrenched in the electronic age and mostly prefers to live in a concrete jungle, the mysterious link between humans and other life forms continues to hold true. Most of our contact with other life forms these days is limited to the fleeting glimpse of a bird overhead, the scurry of a squirrel or chipmunk across our paths, or the companionship of a pet. Yet the role of these life forms is of such great importance that we would not be able to survive without them. Living in harmony with our natural world is the ultimate survival strategy.

Many don't realize but one of the significant ecological catastrophe of this century is near decimation of vulture species, in just a few decades. Though every species has a role in the complex web of life, role of vultures is vital.

I've called this press conference to announce that given the current state of the planet, we are no longer man's best friend.

Bio-diversity refers to genes species and ecosystem of a region. It is the relationship between the species and their habitats. Species are the distinct units of diversity. Each species plays a unique role in ecosystem. Vultures are one such species which plays a very important role in protecting the bio-diversity. Any threat to biodiversity posses immense threat to the survival and well being of mankind.

2.

Vultures

Nature's Perfect Cleaning Crew

Scavengers, especially vultures, provide one of the most important yet under-appreciated ecosystem services of any avian group. Because they feed by scavenging, vultures are highly specialized to rapidly dispose of large carcasses, thus playing a critical role in nutrient cycling, leading other scavengers to carcasses and reducing the risk of contamination by pathogens by quickly consuming decomposing carcasses. Despite the rate at which vultures are declining, little is known about the potential consequences of the widespread disappearance of these scavenging birds on other scavengers and rates of disease transmission at carcasses.

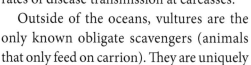

Outside of the oceans, vultures are the only known obligate scavengers (animals that only feed on carrion). They are uniquely adapted to exploit a transient food source that occurs intermittently over large areas. Using gliding flight, vultures take advantage of upward air movements that enable them to travel rapidly over long distances with relatively little energy expenditure. This allows them to search for food efficiently.

They can also search communally by observing other birds from the air. Aerial searching also gives them a considerable advantage over terrestrial scavengers because the latter have limited feeding ranges, higher energy expenditures to locate carcasses, and comparatively poor visibility from the ground.

All vultures locate carcasses using keen eyesight. New World Cathartes vultures also have a well developed sense of smell that is used for locating food in forested areas. Once they have located food, they can travel quickly to reach it, avoiding displacement by larger terrestrial scavengers.

Facultative scavengers, such as hyenas and especially lions, use the activity of vultures to detect carrion, but vultures more than compensate for this competition by arriving rapidly and in large numbers. Vultures are among the largest of flying birds.

Their size allows them to consume more food at each carcass discovery and to carry greater body reserves, which is important given their erratic food supply. A large body also helps them to outcompete smaller scavengers at carcasses and because flight speed is largely determined by body mass; it increases the area that they can search each day.

A recent study using satellite tracking devices determined that the mean foraging range for two immature Cape vultures was an astounding 480,000 km^2 over an eight-month period.

Physiologically, vultures have low pH levels in their digestive tracts (pH 1–2); this destroys most microscopic organisms and

---

I'm amazed that this is the first important study on the disease transmission issue that has shown in my searches. Much like the garbagemen's strike in New York City years ago the loss of one of natures most important cleaners might prove to be the worst ecological disaster of the century. People are quick to complain about the decline of Polor Bears and whales but few seem to see just how serious this problem is. Disease has killed more people worldwide than all wars combined.
~Douglas W Coulter, April 28, 2010

greatly reduces the probability that vultures act as sources of infection at carcasses. Finally, vulture life history is characterized by delayed maturity, low productivity, and relatively high adult survivorship. Vultures and especially condors have some of the lowest reproductive rates among birds, and their populations are particularly vulnerable to high mortality, whether by natural or human causes.

Vultures are considered 'keystone' scavengers, and may therefore play an important role in 'who' comes to carcasses and the amount of interactions they have. In African savannas, apart from small predatory species such as  mongoose and genets, these might include jackals, lions and hyenas. But these types of non-specialist scavengers may not scavenge randomly but on those carcasses where specialists, i.e. vultures, are present in part because the aerial movements of vultures often lead other scavengers to carcasses. Therefore, vulture extinction may lead to a decline in the diversity of species scavenging at carcasses.

Although vulture declines might decrease overall diversity, certain species may benefit. In India, small predators that have benefited from the absence of vultures (e.g. rats, feral dogs) have short lives, high reproductive potential and are important disease reservoirs. Pathogens such as rabies and canine distemper virus can infect and be transmitted by a wide range of host species including

The superior foraging efficiency of avian scavengers is nowhere more apparent than in the Serengeti (Africa), where only vultures have the ability to follow migratory animals over vast distances and benefit from heavy mortality that occurs along the way. It has been estimated that vultures in the Serengeti consume more meat than all the other mammalian carnivores combined.

Vultures in the Serengeti entirely consumed 84% of experimentally placed carcasses before any mammalian scavengers appeared.

mongooses and jackals, whose numbers may also increase at carcasses if vultures become extinct.

Therefore, an increase in scavengers at carcasses could increase rates of disease transmission. This could happen as a result of higher numbers of scavengers that are good disease reservoirs. Also opportunities for disease transmission may increase due to 'more contact between' scavengers.

The vultures can also alert farmers to dead or sick animals, and other scavengers and carnivores to carcasses in the wild.

To conclude:

1) Carcasses decompose more slowly in the absence of vultures.

2) Other scavengers increase and they spend more time in proximity to carcasses because of decreased competition. The lack of facilitation by vultures to find carcasses result in a slower rate at which scavengers locate carcasses. Overall species diversity at carcasses decreases.

Reference:

Ecological implications of vulture extinction on scavengers and disease transmission Darcy Ogada, February 27th, 2010

The acid concentration of the Bearded Vulture stomach has been estimated to be of pH about 1 and large bones will be digested in about 24 hours, aided by slow mixing/churning of the stomach content. The high fat content of bone marrow makes the net energy value of bone almost as good as that of muscle, even if bone is less completely digested. A skeleton left on a mountain will dehydrate and become protected from bacterial degradation and the Bearded Vulture can return to consume the remainder of a carcass even months after the soft parts have been consumed by other animals, larvae and bacteria.

3.

Vulture

An Introduction

V ulture is the name given to two groups of scavenging birds of prey: the New World vultures and the Old World vultures. New World vultures are found in North and South America; Old World vultures are found in Europe, Africa and Asia, meaning that between the two groups, vultures are found on every continent except Australia and Antarctica.

A particular characteristic of many vultures is a bald head, devoid of normal feathers. This helps to keep the head clean when feeding. Research has shown that the bare skin may play an important role in thermoregulation.

Several species have a good sense of smell and are able to smell dead animals from great heights, up to a mile away.

When a carcass has too thick a hide for its beak to open, it waits for a larger scavenger to eat first. Vast numbers have been seen upon battlefields.

They gorge themselves when prey is abundant, until their crop (a pouch in their gullet) bulges, and sit, sleepy or half torpid, to digest their food. They do not carry food to their young in their claws, but disgorge it from their mouth.

These birds are of great value as scavengers, especially in hot regions. Vulture stomach acid is exceptionally corrosive, allowing them to safely digest putrid carcasses infected with Botulinum toxin, hog cholera, and anthrax bacteria that would be lethal to other scavengers.

New World vultures often vomit when threatened or approached. Contrary to some accounts, they don't 'projectile vomit' on their attacker as a deliberate defense, but it does lighten their stomach load to make take-off easier, and the vomited meal residue may distract a predator, allowing the bird to escape.

New World vultures also urinate straight down their legs; the uric acid kills bacteria accumulated from walking through carcasses, and also acts as evaporative cooling.

There are 23 vulture species in the world, and at least one type of vulture is found on every continent except Australia and Antarctica. These are relatively adaptable birds found in a range of habitats, including suburban regions, but even so, 14 species are considered either threatened or endangered.

Vultures are carnivorous and eat carrion almost exclusively. They are able to consume carcasses that may have rotted so much as to be dangerous for other animals. This gives vultures a unique and important ecological niche because they help prevent the spread of diseases from old, rotting corpses.

Vultures have bare heads and often bare necks so that when they feed on rotting carcasses, bacteria and other parasites cannot burrow into their feathers to cause infections. This allows the birds to stay healthier while feeding on material that would easily infect other animals.

There are more vulture species in the Old World, and they are not closely related to New World vultures but are often considered

> *Bearded Vulture, like other vultures it is a scavenger, feeding mostly on the remains of dead animals. It usually disdains the actual meat, however, and lives on a diet that is typically 85–90% bone marrow. This is the only living bird species that specializes in feeding on marrow. The Lammergeier can swallow whole or bite through brittle bones up to the size of a lamb's femur and its powerful digestive system quickly dissolves even large pieces. The Lammergeier has learned to crack bones too large to be swallowed by carrying them in flight to a height of 50–150 m (160–490 ft) above the ground and then dropping them onto rocks below, which smashes them into smaller pieces and exposes the nutritious marrow. They can fly with bones up to 10 cm (3.9 in) in diameter and weighing over 4 kg (8.8 lb), or nearly equal to their own weight. After dropping the large bones, the Bearded Vulture spirals or glides to down to inspect them and may repeat the act if the bone is not sufficiently cracked. This learned skill requires extensive practice by immature birds and takes up to seven years to master. Its old name of Ossifrage ("bone breaker") relates to this habit. More seldom, these birds have been observed to try to break bones (usually of a medium size) by hammering them with their bill directly into rocks while perched.*
>
> *Live prey is sometimes attacked by the Bearded Vulture, with perhaps greater regularity than any other vulture. Among these, tortoises seem to be especially favored depending on their local abundance. Tortoises predated may be nearly as heavy as the predating vulture. When killing tortoise, Bearded Vultures also fly to some height and drop them to crack open the bulky reptiles' hard shells. Golden Eagles have been observed to kill tortoises in the same way. Other live animals, up to nearly their own size, have been observed to be seized and dropped in flight.*
>
> *The Greek playwright Aeschylus was said to have been killed in 456 or 455 BC by a tortoise dropped by a vulture who mistook his bald head for a stone*
>
> *~ Ferguson-Lees, James; Christie, David A. (2001). Raptors of the World*

together because they fill a similar ecological niche.

Vultures have excellent senses of sight and smell to help them locate food, and they can find a dead animal from a mile or more away. Because of this, vultures often have large territories and will spend a lot of time soaring to locate their next meal.

It is said that vultures will circle dying animals waiting to feed. These birds are powerful fliers and will soar on thermals while they look for food, but when they locate a carcass, they will approach it quickly to begin feeding before other predators find it.

Vultures have relatively weak legs and feet with blunt talons, though they do have powerful bills. If a carcass is too stiff for them to rip open, they will wait for another predator to open the flesh before they feed, which is why vultures are often seen in the company of other carrion-eating animals.

A vulture's stomach acid is significantly stronger and more corrosive than that of other animals or birds. This allows these scavengers to feed on rotting carcasses that may be infected with dangerous bacteria, because their stomach acid will kill that bacteria so it does not threaten the vulture.

It is a myth that vultures will prey on healthy livestock, but they are still regularly persecuted by farmers and ranchers who believe the birds to be a threat to their animals.

Vultures urinate on their legs and feet to help cool off on hot days, and their urine also helps kill any bacteria or parasites they've

Scientists have begun to study vultures' unique senses and abilities and are considering using the birds to help find bodies from crimes. Studying how a vulture finds a body and how quickly it can consume the body can be useful for forensic analysis.

In Germany, police have trained turkey vultures to help them find missing people.

picked up from walking through carcasses to help keep the birds healthier.

The Andean condor, found in South America, has the largest wingspan of any vulture in the world, with a spread of 10-11 feet when the bird extends its wings. The crow-sized hooded vulture is the smallest of these birds with a wingspan of only five feet. It is found sub-Saharan Africa.

New World vultures lack a syrinx and are nearly silent. They do not have songs, and their typical vocalizations are limited to grunts, hisses and similar sounds.

Vultures only lay one egg every year or so. A vulture can eat up to 1 kilogram (about 2 pounds) in a single meal (that's over 10% of their body weight).

Vultures have huge ranges with a single individual using all of Kenya, northern Tanzania, and even going into Ethiopia and Sudan. Vultures are the ultimate recyclers – able to strip a carcass in just a few hours, they keep our environment clean and disease free.

Egyptian vultures eat ostrich eggs and actually use rocks or sticks to crack their thick shells.

So that smartness you haven't got. Even of a small bird. And still you are proud of advancement. The vulture goes up and he can see everything but when you go up, aeroplane, up you cannot see where is your home. Is it not? They can find out, four miles, five miles away, where is a corpse, immediately they flock.

~ Srila Prabhupada (Morning Walk -- April 20, 1973, Los Angeles)

Reference:

Ward, J.; McCafferty, D.J.; Houston, D.C.; Ruxton, G.D. (April 2008). "Why do vultures have bald heads? The role of postural adjustment and bare skin areas in thermoregulation". Journal of Thermal Biology 33 (3): 168–173. doi:10.1016/j. jtherbio.2008.01.002.

Lipton, James (1993). An Exaltation of Larks: The Ultimate Edition (third ed.). New York: Penguin Books. p. 275. ISBN 9780140170962. OCLC 29191881.

http://vulturesrock.com/quick-facts/

4.

Vultures

Vanishing In Thin Air

One dramatic wildlife story which receives little public attention is the decline in vulture populations globally. The statistics are quite startling, the impact enormous. It is not only the wildlife eco-system that suffers from this decline but it has massive economic, social and cultural implications for the world.

This declines across the world since last few decades have been among the most dramatic and rapid of any bird species. From

southeast Asia to West Africa, vultures are declining at alarming rates, making them the most threatened functional group of birds.

Historical And Recent Vulture Population Trends

Vulture population declines in Europe and North American likely began as early as the mid-19th century. One hundred years later, some populations of Bearded vultures in Europe and the California condor in North America were already nearing extinction. Further reports of population declines of Cape vultures and of vultures in South Asia testify to the global nature of declines that had already begun prior to the mid-20th century.

In the Middle East, populations of three species are reported to be in decline in the United Arab Emirates, and five species present in Israel are similarly declining. In Europe and North America, which have historically recorded large population declines, the majority of vulture populations are now stable. In vulture-rich regions, large population declines have occurred in recent decades, particularly in Asia and Africa.

Within the Central and South American region, half of the vulture species are estimated to be in decline, though the region has comparatively little published research on vulture populations apart from that on the Andean condor (Vultur gryphus).

Of the 23 known vulture species, the world's only known "obligate scavengers" — animals that only feed on carrion — 14 (61%) are threatened with extinction, with the most rapid declines occurring in "vulture-rich" Asia and Africa, according to a paper published by the New York Academy of Sciences.

Africa

In Africa, recent population collapses have been recorded, particularly in West and East Africa. In West Africa, populations of all vultures except the Hooded vulture have declined by an average of 95% in rural areas over the last 30 years. In protected areas of the Sudanese zone, their collective populations fell by an average of 42% over the same period. In East Africa, vulture declines of 70% were recently recorded over a three-year period in north-central Kenya.

Even the wildlife-rich Masai Mara region has lost an average of 62% of its vultures over the past 30 years, and annual vulture mortality as high as 25% has recently been recorded.

The situation for vultures in North Africa is dire, particularly in Morocco,where two species, Cinereous and Lappetfaced vultures, have been destroyed completely. Others are predicted to follow, and the rest of the region offers little hope for long-term vulture conservation.

Vulture research and conservation have a relatively long history in southern Africa, beginning with the formation of the Vulture Study Group in 1977. That group produced the seminal book 'The Vultures of Africa' and ingrained vulture research within the ornithological community. Vulture populations in the region continue to be the best studied in Africa and rival the level of study of those in Europe and North America. However, there are a few species whose populations continue to decline, and one, the Egyptian vulture, is believed to be extinct as a breeding species in southern Africa.

The Cape vulture is southern Africa's only endemic vulture species and is considered 'Endangered' by the IUCN (International Union for Conservation of Nature). With only 2,900 breeding

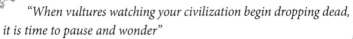

"When vultures watching your civilization begin dropping dead, it is time to pause and wonder"
~ David Brower

pairs, this species has declined across its range and is now extinct as a breeding species in Zimbabwe, Swaziland and now Namibia.

Little was known about vulture species in Uganda apart from some basic monitoring of numbers. In 2011 WCS (Wildlife Conservation Society) started a program to study vultures in the Greater Virunga Landscape, in particular the Lappet-faced vulture which is a threatened species and was identified as one of 13 landscape species for this landscape.

Regular monitoring of vultures at kills in Queen Elizabeth park indicate that there are few vultures of any species and even the most abundant species, the white-backed vulture, numbers less than 350 individuals. In one poisoning event this year over 50 white-backed vultures were killed indicating the level of impact that poisoning of carcasses can have on vulture numbers.

The radio tracking data is indicating where likely breeding sites occur in the landscape and given there are no breeding records of vultures in Uganda it is important to identify these and ensure they are protected. They have also shown that the vultures move long distances between parks, with one individual flying directly to Lake Mburo National park about 100 km east of Queen Elizabeth Park.

In African countries such as Kenya and Namibia, carcasses are laced with the extremely toxic pesticide Furadan by farmers targeting lions and other predatory species that they consider a threat to livestock and humans. Animals that ingest Furadan suffer horrible deaths and then themselves pose a health risk to other scavenger species that ingest their carcass perpetuating this deadly act.

India

From 80 Million To 8 Thousand In 15 Years

Vulture populations in South Asia have incurred the most precipitous and rapid declines ever recorded. In India, Pakistan and Nepal, vulture population has declined by over 99% in last two decades and this alarming trend is continuing. In other Asian countries like Vietnam, Thailand and Laos, dead animals no longer attract vultures, simply because there are not many left.

Indians today can hardly recall the last time that they saw a vulture. In the 1990s, these majestic birds were a common sight in the subcontinent, and would show up wherever there was exposed carrion.

Nine species of vulture can be found living in India. Today, most of them are in danger of extinction. This has not always been the case. In the 1980s there were as many as 80 million white-rumped vultures in India. At that time,  it was the most numerous species of raptor in the world. Today, however, its population numbers only several thousand.

The population of the White-rumped Vulture fell 99.7% between 1993 and 2002. The populations of the Indian Vulture and the Slender-billed Vulture fell 97.4%. Two other species of gyps, the Himalayan Vulture and the Eurasian Griffon, are less affected, the Eurasian Griffon because it only winters in India and has a much smaller initial population, and the Himalayan Vulture, with a similarly small population, because it is exclusively mountain-dwelling.

Vulture populations have continued to decline in India at a rate of between 20% and 40% each year since 2007. The scale is astonishing – for every thousand white-rumped vultures in 1990, only one is alive today. All these species prey on mammals for food.

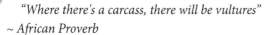

"Where there's a carcass, there will be vultures"
~ *African Proverb*

However, over the years, a number of species like the Indian King, Long-Billed Griffon, India Fulvous, Asian White Rumped and the Himalayan Griffon, which inhabited the Himalayas but were also seen around north India, have become a rare sight these days. Many have simply vanished and may only be found in high mountain ranges.

Studies done by scientist like Dr. Vibhu Prakash (at Keoladeo National Park in Bharatpur in Uttar Pradesh) is indicative of the threat to vultures.

Dr. Prakash has kept track of the bird since 1985. His findings suggests that there were approximately 95 Asian White Rumped vultures on his last count in 1998 against over 2,000 some 14 years ago. The next most common species in the area, the Long- Billed Griffon, hasn't been sighted in the park this year.

It is statistics like these which have prompted scientists to sound the alarm bells. And though, going by the common perception, it is good riddance to the flying scavengers, the fact is that once the vultures disappear, disease and pestilence may follow.

Fortunately for the raptors, several researchers are taking a keen interest in restoring the vulture population. Breeding of Long-billed Vulture at Ramanagaram hills, Karnataka India, a study by S. Subramanya from the University of Agricultural Sciences, Bangalore, is a case in point. The hills of Ramanagaram are located in the south-west of Bangalore and have been a home to critically

During our field study on 9th Sept'07 we had visited a very old khattal (Cow shed) in the steel township of Rourkela (India). Madhusudan Yadav who migrated from Bihar to the steel township some 40 years back and started their milk business. They were throwing the dead cows in the vast open field adjacent to their shed, which were eaten by large number of vultures available till 90's. The Yadav family stated that the vast open field is now being cultivated and has become a paddy growing field. Hence they lack any such facilities for disposing dead cows. Moreover, such disposal of dead animals in the steel city is prohibited. ~ Sonali Patnaik

and globally endangered vulture species for a long time. Recently, eight Longbilled vultures were observed on the ledges of the steep and rocky cliffs dotting the Ramadevarabetta State Forest. The birds seemed healthy, say the scientists and these vultures, according to the Bombay Natural History Society (BNHS), appear to be the only known and last surviving population of the species in inland southern India.

"The survival of this small population of vultures gives hope that its entire population may not have been lost in this part of the country. It is quite possible that this isolated population has been able to resist the effects that have almost decimated the species elsewhere, or may not have been exposed to the same," says Subramanya.

Captive-breeding Programmes

Captive-breeding programmes for several species of Indian vulture have been started. The vultures are long lived and slow in breeding, so the programmes are expected to take decades. Vultures reach breeding age at about 5 years old. It is hoped that captive-bred birds will be released into the wild eventually.

...AND THANK YOU FOR THE INVENT OF THE AUTOMOBILE, WHICH BRINGS US THIS BOUNTIFUL HARVEST, AMEN

In early 2014 the Saving Asia's Vultures from Extinction (Save) programme announced that it expects to start releasing captive-bred birds into the wild by 2016.

"The dramatic decline of vultures in South Asia highlights that we can never be complacent about conservation, even when it comes to 'common' species", said Dr Scott Perkin, Head of IUCN's Biodiversity Conservation Programme, Asia. "The fortunes of a particular species, or even an entire group of species, can change for the worse in a remarkably short period of time."

The Current Status of North American Vultures
By Lloyd F. Kiff

Population trends of three species of North American vultures, the Turkey Vulture, Black Vulture, and California Condor, are reviewed here. Both of the smaller species have undergone dramatic northward range extensions since the 1920s. A decline in numbers occurred in many areas from the 1950s to the early 1970s, coinciding with the period of DDT use in North America., and widespread eggshell thinning was documented.

Based on distributional data from diverse sources, numbers of two species are presently stable but the California condor is struggling to maintain a sustainable population as lead poisoning continues to be the main threat to its survival. Hunters using lead ammunition wound target species thus allowing them to die in a remote location. Condors feeding on the carcass ingest the lead shot and as a result are slowly poisoned to death.

Stability has been achieved by several factors, including increases in the deer population, increased availability of other road-killed animals, reduced pesticide use, reduced human persecution, the  increased number of landfills, and a general warming trend. Climate change in this case, seems to be favoring the species.

Efforts are on to preserve the California Condor, a rare species throughout its recorded history, by a vigorous captive breeding and release programme. Although it is still one of the most endangered species in the world, there is increasing hope that its once all-but-inevitable extinction can be prevented.

Egyptian Vulture

Egyptian Vulture populations have declined in most parts of its range. In Europe and most of the Middle East, populations in 2001 were half of those from 1980. In India, the decline of Egyptian vulture has been rapid with a 35% decrease each year since 1999. In 1967–70, the area around Delhi was estimated to have 12,000–15,000 of these vultures, with an average density of about 5 pairs per 10 km^2.

In Italy, the number of breeding pairs declined from 30 in 1970 to 9 in the 1990s. Nearly all breeding failures were due to human activities. In Spain, which holds about 50% of the European population suggested causes of decline include poisoning by accumulation of lead, pesticides and electrocution. Windfarms also pose a threat. Poorly designed power transmission lines in east Africa electrocute many wintering vultures. Furthermore, studies in Spain suggest that the absorption of veterinary antibiotics suppresses the vultures' innate immunity, making them more prone to infection.

But the main culprit has been a shortage of carrion resulting from new rules for disposal of dead animals following the outbreak of Bovine Spongiform Encephalitis in parts of Europe during 2000.

The population of Egyptian Vultures in the Canary Islands has been isolated from those in Europe and Africa for a significant period of time leading to genetic differentiation. The vulture population there declined by 30% in the ten years between 1987 and 1998. The total population in 2000 was estimated at about 130 individuals, including 25–30 breeding pairs.

In order to provide safe and uncontaminated food for nesting birds, attempts have been made to create "vulture restaurants" where carcasses are made available. However, these interventions may also encourage other opportunist predators and scavengers to concentrate at the site and pose a threat to vultures nesting in the vicinity.

Europe

During the end of the 1960's the future of vultures in France seemed very bleak. The western half of the Pyrenees and Corsica apart, France had virtually lost its big vultures. With a national conservation campaign, a process to restore raptor communities began. The success of Griffon Vulture reintroduction, begun in 1968, in the Massif Central, led in 1990 to the re-establishment of the Griffon Vulture in the Southern Alps and of the Black Vulture in the Massif Central area. Ten years after the start of the Black Vulture programme, the free-ranging population was evolving naturally. International ringing, population monitoring, establishment of feeding sites and rehabilitation centres, and satellite telemetry to determine flight patterns are just a few of the aspects involved in creating an action plan.

The status, distribution and population of the Eurasian Griffon Vulture are extremely contradictory in the western and eastern European range. While populations on the Iberian Peninsula doubled in size, those in the Eastern European/Mediterranean range slightly decreased with local extinctions in many parts. There is no sign of severe decline in vulture populations in the former Soviet Union, suggesting that whatever agent kills birds in India (including lack of food) is either not fatal to northern birds or more likely has not yet impacted these populations.

Reference:

WCS Albertine Rift

Decline of the Vulture, http://www.glo-wild.com/

Dropping dead: causes and consequences of vulture population declines worldwide, Darcy L. Ogada, Felicia Keesing, and Munir Z. Virani

http://en.wikipedia.org/wiki/Egyptian_Vulture

5.

Lack Of Proper Studies

Given the rate at which vultures are declining, there have been surprisingly few studies about the ecological consequences of the widespread disappearance of these scavenging birds. Communities of facultative scavengers are highly structured (not random) and complex, and birds contribute most to this structure because they are the most specialized scavengers.

In West Africa, studies of vultures over the past 40 years are virtually nonexistent though seven years have passed since the

first reports of massive vulture population declines there were first published.

Kenya and Uganda are the only two East African countries where some populations of vultures have been studied and monitored for many decades. In Kenya, two recent studies have shown large declines in most species, and there exist both scientific and anecdotal reports linking the declines to poisoning, primarily to the agricultural pesticide Furadan.

In addition, the vast majority of African governments, with the exception of South Africa, have provided little, if any, support for vulture conservation or have attempted to resolve known vulture threats.

Situation in Asia is no better. Very little is known about the factors responsible for vulture's disappearance. Some studies have been conducted in the last two decades but their conclusions have been questioned by the experts. Their findings, at best, are controversial.

Though the long-term impacts of these declines are not fully understood, ecosystem services provided by vultures have already plummeted and novel research has shown that disease transmission at carcasses may increase.

Reference:

Dropping dead: causes and consequences of vulture population declines worldwide, Darcy L. Ogada, Felicia Keesing, and Munir Z. Virani

6.

Ecosystem service

Ecosystem services are natural processes that benefit humans. The United Nations Millennium Ecosystem Assessment distinguishes four principal types of ecosystem services:

• Provisioning services, such as production of clean water and food;

• Regulating services, obtained through ecosystem processes that regulate climate, water, and human disease;

• Cultural services, such as spiritual enrichment, cognitive development, reflection, recreation, and aesthetics;

• Supporting services, which include all other ecosystem processes, such as soil formation, nutrient cycling, provisioning of habitat, and production of biomass and atmospheric oxygen.

Birds play many roles in ecosystem, such as predators, pollinators, scavengers, seed dispersers, seed predators and ecosystem engineers. *Birds take part in all the four kinds of ecosystem service.*

Scavengers In Ecosystem Service

There are numerous sources of mortality which cause nonpredatory death in animals and birds: death due to old age, malnutrition, disease, parasites, accidents, exposure, and catastrophic events; collisions with human-built structures, collisions with automobiles, poisoning, and pollution.

If sufficient scavengers exist, nonpredatory carcasses will be consumed. But if large obligatory scavengers are absent, carcasses will not be consumed as quick as possible with bacteria dominating the process of decomposition.

Vultures have historically played a very important role in environmental health, by disposing of animal and human remains. Compared to other scavengers, vultures have high mobility, the flight maximizes rapid carrion detection. They can finish the carcasses effectively and efficiently. For thousands of years and in different parts of world, humans have laid out their dead for consumption by scavengers.

Vultures help to dispose cattle carcasses in areas like India where beef eating is forbidden. In most industrial countries such as Germany or China, vultures are extinct. Ecosystem services carried out by vultures in these places have been lost.

In NECROS project of Brandenburg Technical University, the fragmented remains of the food web based on carcasses are studied. What will happen to carcasses of large animals under such conditions? How long will it take to decompose carcasses under different conditions?

Can other scavengers provide the same ecosystem service as vultures?

Methods

Study site is part of one of the largest former military training sites in Brandenburg, Germany. The area selected offers some advantages not found elsewhere: Most of the area is closed to the public, so disturbances by passersby are expected to be few; large vertebrate scavengers such as Wild Boar, Wolf, White Tailed Eagle,

Red Kite, Ravens and others are known to be present. Experiments were performed in all seasons from November 2008 till October 2011. They experimentally laid out some road kills of game.

Carcasses are monitored by three automatic cameras with two of them taking pictures and one taking videos.

Results

They found several influences having impact on the decomposition and consumption of carcasses:

• Season: In summer, carcasses are mainly consumed by arthropods and bacteria. Only Red Fox (Vulpes vulpes) is regularly eating from rotting carcasses, while in winter consumption is done mainly by vertebrates. In winter there are also large flocks of Raven at the carcasses.

• Condition of carcass: It makes a significant difference if the road kill shows open wounds or if the animal died of inside injuries. With no open wounds even White Tailed Eagle with its strong beak has difficulties in opening a carcass.

• Feeding strategy: Ravens do not actually feed at the carcass. They fill their craw with meat, hide it away and come back for more meat.

• Competition: Interspecific and intraspecific competition is more complicated than expected. Competition between vertebrates and bacteria is also remarkable; it seems to follow "first come, first served".

Discussion

When looking at the results it becomes obvious that Ravens play a large role in carcass ecology. However, even large numbers of Ravens cannot contribute to the ecosystem services otherwise provided by vultures.

As Ravens congregate in large flocks only in winter, they fail to provide vulture's ecosystem services year round. Carcasses must have open wounds so that Ravens can get access to the meat.

Consequences of the loss of these services cover more than just lack of food for scavenging animals. It seems plausible, that following the decline of vulture populations in Central Europe, populations of scavenging mammals increased as happened in India some years ago. Foxes are now a common sight even in city centers of large towns.

References:

Scavenging birds and ecosystem services, Experience from Germany, Xiaoying Gu, Rene Krawczynski

[1] Bauer, H.-G., Bezzel, E. & Fiedler, W. (2005): Das Kompendium der Vögel Mitteleuropas. Band 1: Nonpasseriformes – Nichtsperlingsvögel. AULA: 1 – 808.

[2] Green, R.E., Newton, I., Shultz, S., Cunningham, A.A.,Gilbert,M.,Pain, D.J., Prakash,V. (2004): Diclofenac-poisoning as a cause of vulture population declines across the Indian subcontinent. J. Appl. Ecol. 41, 793-800.

[3] Krawczynski, R. & Wagner, H.-G. (2008): Leben im Tod – Tierkadaver als Schlüsselelemente in Ökosystemen. – Naturschutz & Landschaftsplanung 40 (9): 261-264.

[4] Pain, D.J., Cunningham, A.A., Donald, P.F.,Duckworth, J.W.,Houston,D.C.,Katzner, T.,Parryjones, J., Poole, C., Prakash, V., Round, P., Timmins, R. (2003): Causes and effects of temporospatial declines of Gyps-vultures.

[5] Rodriguez, J.P., Beard, T.D., Agard, J.R.B., Bennett,E., Cork, S., Cumming, G.,Deane, D., Dobson, A.P., Lodge, D.M., Mutale, M., Nelson, G.C., Peterson, G.D., Ribeiro,T., Carpenter, S.R., Pingali, P.L., Bennett, M.E., Zurek, M.B.(2005):

Chapter 12:Interactions among ecosystem services. In Ecosystems and Human well-being: scenarios, volume 2 (2005).

[6] Markandya, A., Taylor, T., Longo, A., Murty, M.N., Murty, S., Dhavala, K. (2008): Counting the cost of vulture decline-An appraisal of the human kealth and other benefits of vultures in India. (Available at http://www.scribd.com/doc/49834172/Counting-the-cost-ofvulture- decline%E2%80%94An-appraisal-of-the-human-healthand- other-benefits-of-vultures-in-India).

[7] Swan, G. E., Cuthbert, R., Quevedo, M., Green, R. E., Pain, D. J., Bartels, P., Cunningham, A. A., Duncan, N., Meharg, A. A., Oaks, J. L., Parry-Jones, J., Shultz, S., Taggart,

M. A., Verdoorn, G. & Wolter, K. (2006): Toxicity of diclofenac to Gyps vultures. Biol. Letters 2006 2: 279 – 282.

[8] Whelan, C.J., Wenny, D.G., Marquis, R.J.(2008): Ecosystem Services Provided By Birds. (Available at http://onlinelibrary.wiley.com/doi/10.1196/annals.1439.003/abstract).

Chair General Ecology, Brandenburg Technical University, Cottbus, Germany

7.

Scavenging Birds And Ecosystem Services

Experience from Germany

Vultures are extinct in industrial countries like Germany mainly due to prosecution and lack of food. Extinction of vultures occurred at several decades ago.

Rabies was a major risk to public health in Germany until the disease was eradicated by vaccinating foxes. Without competition by vultures and without rabies causing death among foxes, their population increased tremendously and foxes are now regarded as a threat for ground breeding birds.

Thus Germany's interference in the carrion food web by vaccinating foxes have caused several negative effects.

In the NECROS project of BTU Cottbus (Germany) the fragmented remaining food web based on carcasses has been studied.

As part of the study, road kills of game, mainly roe deer and wild boar, were deposited in a nature reserve to carry out field experiments. Carcasses were monitored by automatic cameras. One of the main aims was to find out what happens to the carrion food web with only some vertebrate scavengers around and no vultures at all.

Results showed that compared to complete ecosystems with large predators and vultures, the rudimentary food web based on carrion in Germany cannot provide the desirable ecosystem services.

Reference:

Scavenging birds and ecosystem services, Experience from Germany, Xiaoying Gu, Rene Krawczynski

8.

Vultures

In Tradition And Culture

In the Vedic scripture Ramayana, Jatayu was the king of vultures. He risked his life and fought with Ravana, the ten headed demon, to save Goddess Sita. There is a shrine being built to Jatayu on a mountain in Kerala that will be one day the largest functioning statue in the world.

In Tibetan culture, vultures perform very important sky burials. In this mountainous terrain, it is hard to find suitable land to bury the dead or sufficient fuel wood to cremate the dead. Vultures here provide a natural disposal system.

India's Parsee community also follows sky burial system for its dead. Sky burials date from the eighth century when the Parsees, also called Zoroastrians, were forced by their Muslim conquerors in Persia to leave their dead unburied.

Parsees believe that in the sky burial the corpse is prevented from polluting the sacred elements of fire, air, water and earth. In Zoroastrianism, water (apo, aban) and fire (atar, adar) are agents of ritual purity, and the associated purification ceremonies are considered the basis of ritual life. In Zoroastrian cosmogony, water and fire are respectively the second and last primordial elements to have been created, and scriptures consider fire to have its origin in the waters.

The use of the vulture as a symbol of royalty in Egyptian culture and their protection by Pharaonic law made the species common on the streets of Egypt and gave rise to the name "Pharaoh's Chicken".

A southern Indian temple at Thirukalukundram near Chengalpattu was famed for a pair of Egyptian vulture birds that reputedly visited the temple for "centuries".

These birds were ceremonially fed by the temple priests and arrived before noon to feed on offerings made from rice, wheat, ghee, and sugar. Although

The New York Times reports how two new aviaries for vultures, brought to the brink of extinction, are being built, so that the ancient tradition of leaving corpses in Towers of Silence to be picked apart by the giant scavenging birds can resume.

The plan is the result of six years of negotiations between Parsi leaders and the Indian government to revive a centuries-old practice that seeks to protect the ancient elements — air, earth, fire and water — from being polluted by either burial or cremation. And along the way, both sides hope the effort will contribute to the revival of two species of vulture that are nearing extinction. The government would provide the initial population of birds.

The stone towers are open-air auditoriums containing three concentric rings of marble slabs — an outer ring for dead men, middle ring for deceased women and inner ring for dead children. For centuries, bodies left on the slabs were consumed within hours by neighborhood vultures, with the bones left in a central catchment to leach into the soil.

normally punctual, the failure of the birds to turn up was attributed to the presence of "sinners" among the onlookers.

References:

Neelakantan 1977.

Siromoney 1977.

http://en.wikipedia.org/wiki/Egyptian_Vulture

http://www.ncbi.nlm.nih.gov/pmc/articles/PMC1618889/

9.

Lack Of Food

The Most Important And Neglected Reason

For The Decline Of Vulture Population

Disappearance of vultures is attributed to many factors but one of the most important factor - lack of food, is often downplayed.

Disappearance of vultures roughly follows the timeline of meat consumption in human society. With the advent of mechanized transport and refrigeration, 20th century saw a global rise in meat consumption and trade. International marketing networks in animal products were established. Meat consumption rose many fold. Mechanized industrial slaughterhouses had sophisticated waste treatment facilities. By middle of the 19th century, very few domestic animals were dying natural death. Most of them started ending up in slaughterhouses before the end of their natural life span. Even in countries like India where people are predominantly vegetarian, governments started exporting meat (By the way, India is the largest exporter of beef in the world today). Where is the possibility of a decent meal for the vulture?

No matter how hungry the vulture, it will never eat grass.
(African Proverb)

At the same time, wildlife population plummeted due to deforestation, poaching and loss of habitat. This also didn't help the cause of vulture survival.

Recently in last one decade, across the European Union scavengers are threatened with extinction owing to a well-intended but ill-conceived regulation introduced by the EU government in Brussels.

This regulation (1774/2002) dates from the year 2002, where the fear of BSE or "mad cow disease" was rampant in Europe and the EU, which issued a number of new directives to protect the population as much as possible from exposure to the epidemic.

I know you're hungry, but you can see for yourself that dinner is not ready: It's still moving...

As part of these new regulations, it was decreed that dead cows, sheep, goats and horses would need to be disposed of in a licensed animal disposal facilities.

Before this new regulations it was normal that when farmed animals died in remote and inaccessible pastures, particularly in Mediterranean countries, they were either left where they were or were taken to designated carcass dumps.

Eagles, vultures, wolves and brown bears, insects etc. would scavenge on the carrion. Nowadays this is not possible anymore: all dead animals, if owned by somebody, have to be taken away from their environment, which heavily impacts the population of scavengers.

> *"... the way we eat represents our most profound engagement with the natural world. Daily, our eating turns nature into culture, transforming the body of the world into our bodies and minds."*
> ~ Michael Pollan

Vultures are suffering as a result of the new food shortage. In May 2003 the EU introduced an exception that permits animal carcasses to be laid out in special, fenced-off feeding areas. But there are not nearly enough of these feeding stations and scavengers are struggling.

This lack of food has led a number of vultures in Europe to change their eating habits. Although the birds have occasionally attacked newborn, sick and unmoving animals, this has become far more frequent in recent years.

Farmers who were previously happy to leave dead animals to the scavengers are less keen to see the birds come after living animals .

Spain - A Case Study

In Spain, before the onset BSE (Bovine spongiform encephalopathy) many Spanish villages used traditional "muladares" to dump dead animals. This, along with wide spread hunting, helped to sustain Spain's large vulture population.

The arrival of BSE saw the introduction of new rules banning this practice and obliging farmers (and hunters) to clear up any dead animals as quickly as possible. Inevitably, this meant a sharp reduction in the availability of carrion and a threat to the continued existence of vultures.

Accordingly, "vulture restaurants" - fenced areas where carefully monitored carcasses (often horses or mules which are not vulnerable to BSE) - were created to provide these scavengers with a regular food supply. These feeding stations have since become the main food source for all avian scavengers. This has doubtless helped them to maintain, even increase, their numbers. It's not all good news though.

Evidently, their use has meant an increase in competition in the more solitary bearded vulture and a consequent decline in breeding success. Similarly, the increase in crows opportunistically using the 'restaurants' has cause a sharp decrease in the breeding success of passerines (a class of birds) near these sites.

Furthermore, it's altered the habits of vultures who, rather than cruise the skies in search of food, are now more likely to loaf around near the more certain sources of food. There's also been a worryingly large increase in the levels of veterinary drugs in Spain's vultures. Presumably, this reflects the change in the origins of available carcasses and it's not yet clear what the long term impact of this might be.

Hunger has driven many vultures out of countries like Spain and into areas where they are not native. Flocks of the large scavengers have been sighted in Germany, Belgium and France. A perceived positive trend of vulture habitat expansion in Europe may actually be hiding severe food shortages in the natural strongholds of these birds.

The situation for flightless scavengers such as brown bears is even worse than that of vultures, as migration into new areas of Europe is much more problematic.

The vulture embraced the chicken until its last breath.
(Russian Proverb) - More Russia

Because many species of vultures are social, vultures are highly effected by shortfall in carcass supply. The entire colony is affected by lack of food. They mostly feed in groups.

A group of vultures is called a committee, venue or volt.

In many countries, people have set up vulture restaurants or feeding sites where carcasses can be left out for vultures. These restaurants help to ensure that vultures have enough food and can help them to avoid contaminated carcasses. In South Africa these are even visited by tourists who enjoy watching the vultures feed.

India - Vulture's Share Exported

In countries like India, the slaughterhouses used to dispose their wastes in dump sites and vultures used to feed there. But in recent years, modernization of slaughterhouses has taken its toll.

These slaughterhouses have sophisticated waste disposal systems and they utilize every bit of animal parts, thus leaving the vultures high and dry. Also the slaughterhouses can no longer afford an image where vultures are hovering over. They have to be more inconspicuous and blend in with their surrounding.

It is important to understand why India formerly had such large vulture populations. Vultures are generally very dependent on human activities (culture, society, etc.). The Hindu culture in India is particularly favorable to vultures, and represents 80% of the country's population. Hindus do not eat cows, which they consider sacred. Cows are used, however, for milk products and as beasts of burden. When a cow dies, it is not eaten by humans, but by vultures. Of the estimated 500 million head of cattle in India, only 4% were destined for consumption by humans as meat. Vultures constituted

India's optimal natural animal disposal system, processing carcasses even in cities. Up to 15,000 vultures have been observed at the carcass depositories of New Delhi. But this is all history now.

In early 90's, government of India realized the potential of beef export. Instead of feeding vultures, politicians thought to export carcasses and earn foreign exchange to fatten their Swiss bank accounts. Many slaughterhouses were established, subsidies were provided on animal transport, meat storage and shipping. Training institutes were opened to train slaughterhouse workers. The entire government machinery was mobilized to this effect. Beef export and increasing domestic meat consumption became the single most important national priority of the Indian government.

This is roughly the time Vultures started disappearing from Indian skies. In 2013, India officially became the largest beef exporter in the world. International community is shocked that a nation in which cow slaughter is officially prohibited and is an utter anathema to the majority of the population, will overtake these three icons (Australia, Brazil and US) of cattle ranching and beef eating.

With all their food, neatly packed and sent away in ships, Indian vultures stand no chance of surviving here.

The physician prescribes the medicine, the vulture waits for the body.
(Turkish Proverb)

USA - A Mixed Picture

In some regions of USA, the availability of eligible carcasses probably increased as a result of human activities. As soon as automobiles became part of the American scene in the early part of the this century, vultures began to profit from the new availability of road-killed creatures, despite occasionally becoming road kills themselves (Sutton 1928).

Throughout the western portion of the United States, for Turkey and Black Vultures, cattle have become a modern staple of their diet, but changes in ranching practices, including the increased use of feedlots and the tendency of some ranchers to promptly remove cow carcasses from the open range, have led to a decline in the availability of this food source. This may have contributed to a lower density of these species in some western states, as suggested for Texas by Porter and White (1977), for Utah by Taylor (1986), and for Arizona by Rea (1998b), but it has no doubt been partially compensated by the increase in landfills and roadkills.

References:

The Current Status of North American Vultures, Lloyd F. Kiff

http://www.lhnet.org/introduction-on-vultures/

Indian statistics, 2001

Oaks et al, 2003

10.

Diclofenac

A Hype And An Alibi

As The Sole Reason For Vulture's Extinction

Diclofenac is a 'nonsteroidal anti-inflammatory 'drug taken or applied to reduce inflammation and as an analgesic reducing pain in certain conditions. It is supplied as or contained in medications under a variety of trade names.

In the United Kingdom, India, Brazil, and the United States, diclofenac may be supplied as either the sodium or potassium salt; in China, it is most often supplied as the sodium salt, while in some other countries it is only available as the potassium salt.

This drug has been squarely blamed for decimation of vulture species in South Asia by Dr. Lindsay Oaks and his team in 2003. South Asia lost tens of millions of vultures in just one decade. Diclofenac is a common anti-inflammatory drug administered to livestock. Following this report, the drug was taken off the market in India in March 2006. Nepal and Pakistan followed the suit shortly afterwards.

Government reports make no mention of starvation, an important factor in vulture deaths. This is a dangerous and ecocidal move, to neglect so many important reasons and go after only one. Many experts suggest the hand of meat export lobby in putting the blame squarely on Diclofenac. That way they are absolved of any responsibility for taking away the vulture's share and thus causing an ecological disaster. There are multiple explanations for the declining population of vultures and it's dangerous to depend on just one.

A Times Of India Report dated Sep 11, 2013, confirms this:

Diclofenac Not The Sole Cause Of Vulture Deaths, Say Experts

Vijay Pinjarkar, Times Of India (TNN), Sep 11, 2013

Nagpur: Use of diclofenac in animals has been reported to have led to a sharp decline in the vulture population in the Indian subcontinent and their numbers declined by 95% in the last decade. But experts deny that the painkiller drug is not the sole reason for extinction of vultures.

At a forum organized to mark International Vulture Awareness Day 2013, head, Nagpur Veterinary College medicine department, Dr N P Dakshinkar, said, "There cannot be one reason for extinction of vultures. Diclofenac may be one of the reasons."

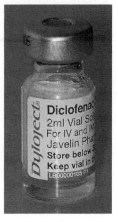

Bird expert and former honorary wildlife warden Gopal Thosar observed that starvation is the main cause of vulture deaths.

Thosar said earlier when a cattle died, farmers used to throw the carcass on the village outskirts where vultures used to feast on it. But nowadays as cattle are being taken away by butchers, vultures have been deprived of food. In Vidarbha, there is no evidence to prove that vultures died of diclofenac.

Raptor scientist and National Association for Welfare of Animals and Research secretary Dr Ajay Poharkar, who is working for vulture conservation in Gadchiroli, has scientifically established that vultures died of avian malaria in the tribal district. His research paper on 'Vulture deaths and theory of malarial deaths' have been internationally recognized.

Dr Poharkar had also pioneered the idea of 'vulture restaurant' in Gadchiroli, when other states were just contemplating about it.

[Emphasis added]

Pune based NGO Ela Foundation and the National Institute of Virology (NIV) have recently published a research paper that analyses the cause of drastic fall in the vulture population of India. While many believe the main reason for the deaths is use of Diclofenac, a chemical that is fatal to the birds, the research papers suggests other reasons too.

"It has been reported that the two species of vultures, the Oriental White-backed Vulture and the Long-billed Vulture Gyps indicus, have declined in population by more than 90 per cent throughout India. It was believed that morbid birds exhibit signs of illness (neck drooping syndrome) for approximately 30 days prior to death. We undertook further investigations on this bird, as vultures are threatened with extinction and, therefore, it is of utmost importance to investigate the causes of morbidity and mortality in these birds," says ornithologist Satish Pande from the Ela Foundation, which is also the principal investigator.

Mr. Pande says, "One major reason is shortage of food. As per government's directions under the Gram Swachata Abhiyan, livestock carcasses have to be buried and not left outside. This has led to a major reduction in food for vultures."

It is sure that vultures are going to be extinct soon if we don't find out the proper cause and take preventive measures soon. Even in my own locality village, when I was a kid of 10-11 years old there used to be a lot of vultures in a tree. But now I find not a single vulture in whole of my state leave alone my village. I haven't seen one perhaps in the last one and half decade or perhaps two decade. This is very serious. Must be that they have gone because now there is hardly any food available for them. In earlier days, there were a lot of cattle in the villages whereas nowadays its hard to find any even in villages where the villagers are farmers. Raring of cattle should be encouraged. After all they give good manure and milk products too.

~ James Darma

The people of Ela Foundation do not believe that this chemical is harming the vultures as much as projected. This is because the shelf life of Diclofenac is 6 hours and if the vultures do eat the carcasses of animals who have been administered the drug, the chances of the chemical reaching their body is very less.

Pande believes that though the use of the chemical may be one of the causes for the vulture deaths, it may not be the sole reason as the drug has also been banned from use and its usage has reduced if not totally stopped.

I blame it on the GPS-System myself:
Hardly anybody gets lost around here anymore...

"Diclofenac led them to be afflicted with a disease called Gout, leading to organ dysfunction. The authorities therefore banned the drug. But the vultures are on the decline. Diclofenac poisoning is therefore not the only cause. Only few vultures have hitherto been known to have died of diclofenac poisoning. The decline has therefore been due to a number of causes," says Pande.

Paper titled 'Diclofenac disposition in Indian cow and goat with reference to Gyps vulture population declines', by MA Taggart et al interestingly indicates that despite mounting evidence regarding

I have been working on vultures in southern U.P. and Northern M.P. since last 6 years. Vultures have declined and are now confined to protected areas. When surveyed it was found that the villagers were too poor to use diclofenac for their cattle.....more over if vultures died in such large numbers than why haven't the villagers seen any carcasses? When asked about the sightings of dead carcasses the answer was they haven't seen any.

~Sonika, April 18, 2011

the role of diclofenac in affecting a population decline in vultures, its importance as the cause for the decline in vulture population in India, has been questioned. In certain regions of the country, vultures can still be found in areas where diclofenac is likely to be used. Likewise, other potential agents of decline have also been suggested as likely to reduce the survival and nesting success of vultures.

Farmers in rural areas are increasingly unable to maintain cattle as the fodder prices go through the roof. Tractors are replacing bulls who are becoming more rare and expensive. Government's policy of encouraging beef export finally leaves very little for the vultures. Vultures need to eat at least once in three days. Such luxury is simply not available these days.

No food - any one with a little common sense can see the reason for vulture's disappearance. It is not a rocket science and does not need a plethora of research reports and high sounding theories.

It's time we admit that we are eating more of what rightfully belongs to them.

References:

Salmann AR (1986). "The history of diclofenac". Am. J. Med. 80 (4B): 29–33. doi:10.1016/0002-9343(86)90076-8.

Six Reasons Why Vultures may be dying in India, Atula Gupta

Vijay Pinjarkar, Times Of India (TNN), Sep 11, 2013

http://www.novartis.com/about-novartis/company-history/index.shtml

http://www.pubmedcentral.nih.gov/articlerender.fcgi?artid=1434053

11.

Vulture Deaths

Reasons Other Than Dietary Insufficiencies.

This chapter deals with factors responsible for vulture deaths other than food shortage. All these factors are man made. Extinction of vultures has nothing to do with processes of extinction that exist in nature.

Pesticide And Chemical Poisoning

A relatively less researched reason for the dwindling population is the rampant use of pesticides in farming. Recently, the Centre of Science and Environment (CSE) in India undertook a study of the eating habits of vultures around Delhi and Uttar Pradesh. The study revealed high incidence of deadly chemicals like DDT, aldrin, dieldrin and BHC in the stomach of these birds.

The theory is that the cattle imbibe these pesticides from the grass and other green vegetation. When the cattle die, vultures ingest these chemicals in the flesh.

Scientists feel the quantities of pesticides found in carcass may or may not be the cause of the death of cattle but once they are consumed by the comparatively small-framed vultures, they lead to disorders in their reproductive organs, even causing thinning of their egg shells which further results in high mortality rates.

For most experts this is worrisome, because vultures lay no more than two or three eggs and that too just once a year. Researchers studying their dwindling population have found that pesticide residue causes almost a 20 percent thinning in the egg-shells, making them vulnerable to the elements of nature, premature hatching and also falling prey to predatory birds.

In India, vulture populations were reported dying out a few years ago in Keoladeo National Park in western Rajasthan state, scientists attributed this to indiscriminate use of the pesticide DDT, both as an  agricultural pesticide and in malaria control. In India, these chemicals have entered the food chain. Tests carried out by the Indian Council of Medical Research (ICMR) in Delhi showed that lactating mothers were passing unacceptable amounts of DDT to infants in breast milk. Other tests showed unacceptably high amounts of DDT in the cows, which were left largely to vultures. Experiments have shown that DDT can interfere with bird reproduction by affecting the embryonic development or by reducing the thickness of eggshells.

The postmortem findings of many vultures carcasses have shown death due to visceral gout. Visceral gout is an accumulation of uric acid within the tissue and on the surface of internal organs. Visceral gout is caused by renal failure, which is known to occur as a result of metabolic infections or toxic diseases. Sick vultures in India become increasingly weak over days or weak before death and are seen to head droop / neck drooping as they become further incapacitated. The presence of an infections disease or avian influenza virus is another major cause of large scale death of vultures.

Human persecution

Direct human persecution of these vulture species has taken the usual forms, including shooting, trapping, and deliberate poisoning. In the United States, throughout the first half of the present century, many ranchers and farmers associated Turkey and Black Vultures with the spread of livestock diseases, especially anthrax, and therefore often sought to eliminate them, usually by trapping. In addition, there were also more valid concerns about Black Vulture attacks on calves and other newborn livestock. In some regions there were large-scale government-sponsored and private programmes to eliminate problem

"REMEMBER, CLASS ... EVERY DAY YOUR DIET SHOULD INCLUDE SOMETHING FROM THE TWO BASIC FOOD GROUPS."

vultures. According to Snyder and Rea (1998), literally hundreds of thousands of Black and Turkey Vultures were eliminated by trapping in Florida and Texas during the 1940s and 1950s. There are still some locally based government-sanctioned removal episodes, usually in response to Black Vulture livestock depredations. Otherwise, there appears to be little direct persecution of either species, and both are now protected by the Migratory Bird Treaty Act, a treaty between the United States, Canada, and Mexico.

By and large, however, shooting and directed poisoning episodes are increasingly rare throughout most of the ranges of these species and will probably continue to decline as a result of changing American attitudes toward wildlife and an increasing trend toward corporate agriculture in the United States and Canada. There is a low cost: benefit ratio for large corporations in shooting or poisoning vultures in this era of heightened environmental awareness in North America. Most find it more acceptable to endure occasional minor losses or inconveniences from the vultures than to generate disproportionate negative publicity and public outcry by shooting them.

In Africa and Europe, the deliberate poisoning by humans of carnivores, which kills scavengers as well as the intended victims, is likely the most widespread cause of vulture poisoning. Carnivore poisoning continues to be common, especially in Europe and Africa. In Europe, poisoning is used to kill predators of game animals (e.g., rabbits, pheasants, and partridges) because hunters believe carnivores such as foxes and mongooses reduce their hunting success. In both Europe and Africa, poisoning is used to "protect" livestock from predators. In Europe, it is regarded as the first option to deter carnivores from attacking livestock, while in Africa poisoning is largely used to avenge the killing of livestock.

Because of the gregarious nature of vultures, large numbers of the animals can be poisoned at once. "Vultures are incredibly social when eating," Diekmann explains. "Numbers are security, so they will often wait until there are hundreds of birds to begin eating. A lot of followers and not many leaders. The problem is that if a carcass is poisoned you can kill 50 to 500 birds at once. I cannot think of any other species that this is possible with."

In India a number of tribes in Andhra Pradesh, Karnataka and Maharashtra eat vulture meat. But what is more worrisome is the fact that villagers view these carnivores as aggressive predators with a penchant to swoop and lift their livestock.

Though this may not be true, elaborate traps are laid out to kill these vultures, the commonest being to mix lethal poison in a carcass which kills these birds instantly.

The increasing air traffic in big cities too has taken its toll. With the number of bird hits going up, the civil aviation and air force authorities have special squads to hunt down vultures which, because of their size, are a major threat to flying aircraft.

In Africa, continued use of vulture parts in traditional medicine and sorcery is impacting vulture population. In India, vulture deaths have occurred during the kite flying festivals when they get entangled in the corrosive thread.

Loss of Habitat

All over the world, human encroachment on natural world is taking place at an increasing pace. This is affecting all forms of life on the planet. Vultures are no exception.

Rapid urbanization is one such factor. For example, increasing urbanization of coastal southern California, once a stronghold of Turkey Vulture populations, has contributed to a decline in numbers there (Garrett & Dunn 1981, Unitt 1984). Another negative anthropogenic effect on vulture habitat has been a decline in the Southeast in the availability of suitable nesting sites, principally large hollow trees, for Black Vultures as a result of modern timbering practices (Jackson 1983, Robbins & Easterla 1992).

In West Africa, habitat loss and degradation are suspected to have played roles in the dramatic declines (of over 98%) of large vultures outside of protected areas where human population growth has been very rapid.

Mass drowning of vultures (of up to 38 birds at a time) has also been reported, particularly in semiarid areas of SouthAfrica where the birds enter artificial reservoirs presumably to bathe or cool off, only to be unable to extricate themselves due to vertical reservoir walls.

In India, observations of vulture breeding colonies indicated that in some areas there had been localized losses of nesting sites, with felling of nesting trees and quarrying of some cliffs, as also reported around Jodhpur, Rajasthan (Chhangani and Mohnot, 2004).

Electrocution

The researchers in India rescued an Oriental White-backed Vulture, which was found in an open field at Bhangaon village in Shrigonda taluka. They conducted studies on the bird and found that it was emaciated but was not poisoned.

Shailesh Pawar, a scientist, said, "Blood, serum, cloacal, faecal and tracheal swabs of the bird were collected and tested at the National Institute of Virology (NIV). There was no evidence of blood parasites or blood infection like malaria or Avian Influenza viruses. It was a case of starvation"

When the bird was eventually fed and released, it got electrocuted from electricity wires almost 60 km away from the point of release. The researchers thus believe that electrocution is responsible for many vulture deaths because the larger the bird and its wing span, the higher the chances of electrocution.

The Cape Griffon vulture, the largest bird of its kind in Africa, is also one of the most endangered. Listed as vulnerable to extinction by the World Conservation Union it has suffered a significant population decline over the past few decades. Among the dangers faced by the Capes, which are confined to a small area of south and southwest Africa, is electrocution on power lines.

Recent proliferation of wind farms as a source of green energy production also has had adverse effects. In recent studies, Griffon vultures suffered very high levels of mortality after collision with wind turbine blades. Given the rapid increase in the development of green technology and electricity, these threats are likely to increase in coming decades.

Secondary Poisoning

In North America, according to Snyder and Snyder (1991), Turkey Vultures are relatively insensitive to natural pathogens and some rodenticides but quite sensitive to other poisons, including cyanide and strychnine, which were formerly used widely to poison coyotes and other perceived threats to cattle and sheep. These two vulture species like California Condors, may also be unusually sensitive to lead poisoning, which they can obtain in the form of bullet fragments in shot mammals carcasses and gutpiles. Little is known of the effects of range poisons on North American vulture populations, but it could have been considerable during former eras, when setting out poisoned carcasses for vermin was a widespread practice, and hunting was more pervasive.

References:

Birds of prey of the Indian subcontinent, Rishad Naoroji, 2007, Om Books international

Pocket Guide to the Birds of the Indian Subcontinent, Richard Grimmet/Carol Inskipp/Tim Inskip, 1998, Oxford

The Current Status of North American Vultures, Lloyd F. Kiff

Six Reasons Why Vultures may be dying in India, Atula Gupta

12.

Extinction Of Vultures

Impact And Consequences

The story of the declining vultures is yet another reminder that ecosystems are fragile, interconnected and delicately balanced. Destroying a species can affect our own health, our environment, and even our culture in ways that are near impossible to predict.

D. L. OGADA writes in his Paper, Effects of Vulture Declines on Facultative Scavengers and Potential Implications for Mammalian Disease Transmission :

"Vultures (Accipitridae and Cathartidae) are the only known obligate scavengers. They feed on rotting carcasses and are the most threatened avian functional group in the world. Possible effects of vulture declines include longer persistence of carcasses and increasing abundance of and contact between facultative scavengers at these carcasses. These changes could increase rates of transmission of infectious diseases, with carcasses serving as

hubs of infection. To evaluate these possibilities, we conducted a series of observations and experimental tests of the effects of vulture extirpation on decomposition rates of livestock carcasses and mammalian scavengers in Kenya. We examined whether the absence of vultures changed carcass decomposition time, number of mammalian scavengers visiting carcasses, time spent by mammals at carcasses, and potential for disease transmission at carcasses (measured by changes in intraspecific contact rates). In the absence of vultures, mean carcass decomposition rates nearly tripled. Furthermore, the mean number of mammals at carcasses increased 3-fold (from 1.5 to 4.4 individuals/carcass), and the average time spent by mammals at carcasses increased almost 3-fold (from 55 min to 143 min). There was a nearly 3-fold increase in the mean number of contacts between mammalian scavengers at carcasses without vultures. These results highlight the role of vultures in carcass decomposition and level of contact among mammalian scavengers. In combination, our findings lead us to hypothesize that changes in vulture abundance may affect patterns of disease transmission among mammalian carnivores."

India - A Case Study

The sudden collapse of the natural animal disposal system in India has had obvious and multiple consequences. These points hold good for other places too.

> *Without vultures South Africa would see animal disease "spread like wildfire", first through the game parks and conservation areas and then, from there, into livestock, affecting the country's meat, dairy and wool production, says BirdLife South Africa director Gerhard Verdoorn.*
>
> *"It would be a disaster (if South Africa lost its vultures). They are right on top of the food chain and my gut feeling is that their loss would have a serious impact on the entire ecology," says Prof Verdoorn. The chemistry professor and raptor expert was at the weekend's official launch of a R500,000 "vulture restaurant" at the Golden Gate Highlands National Park.*

Environmental Impact

To begin with, as carcasses once eaten by vultures now rot in village fields, drinking water has become seriously contaminated.

Secondly, the disappearance of vultures has allowed other species, such as rats and wild dogs, to take their place. These newly abundant scavengers, however, are not as efficient as vultures. While a vulture's metabolism is in fact a true "dead-end" for pathogens, dogs and rats instead become carriers of the pathogens.

India today has an estimated 25 million wild dogs, the largest population of carnivores in the world.

The resulting multiplication of feral dogs in India and Pakistan has caused a multiplication of leopards feeding on those dogs and invading urban areas looking for dogs as prey, resulting in occasional attacks on human children.

Sanitary Impact

These feral dogs, carrying diseases from rotting carcasses (rabies, anthrax, plague, etc.), are directly or indirectly responsible for thousands of human deaths. Today in India, 30,000 people die from rabies each year, more than half the world's total. A person is bitten every 2 seconds, and one dies from rabies every 30 minutes. 70% of the victims are children under the age of 15.

Water contamination is also a worry for authorities as rotting meat degrades & enters the water table. In a country where water is a scarce and valued resource this has potentially dire consequences.

Economic Impact

Treating these diseases is extremely costly for the Indian government and people. Around half a million Indians are treated for rabies each year, at a cost of 1500 rupees per person, while the minimum wage in India is 600 rupees per month. The poorest citizens do not have access to this care, even though they are the most afflicted. According to a study led by M. K. Sudarsham in 2007, medical care to treat animal bites costs India over 25 million dollars.

In addition to the cost of care, India faces the problem of managing these disease-carrying wild dogs. At first they were killed without restriction, but organizations for animal rights brought pressure to prevent indiscriminate killing. The new solution is to vaccinate and to sterilize the animals, and the cost is enormous.

It is the females that must be sterilized, as a single non-castrated male can mate with numerous females and father hundreds of puppies (a female can give birth to up to 20 in a year). The logistics of this program have run into various difficulties: lack of material, of personnel, difficulty in capturing animals etc.

These sterilizations are, however, the best method of controlling wild dog populations without completely eliminating them, which would allow other undesirable species (monkeys, rats, etc.) to take their place. If the cost of treating animal bites is considered along with the expense of managing the wild dogs, researchers have shown that the decline of vultures is costing India 34 billion US dollars every year.

Neeta Shah, an advocacy officer with the Vulture Advocacy Programme initiated by the Bombay Natural History Society

(BNHS), points out that with the absence of vultures, expensive alternate methods of carcass disposal have been necessitated. Many cattle owners who can ill afford it now must pay for carcass burial or cremation services.

In Nepal, the economic benefits of conserving vultures were estimated at $6.9 million, and interviews in communities within Important Bird Areas showed they were considered significantly beneficial to humans.

In Uganda, Hooded vultures used to consume primarily internal organs from diseased animals thrown from abbatoirs, thereby saving local councils the expense of a more sophisticated system of collection and disposal of refuse.

Cultural Impact

While the sanitary, ecological, and economic consequences are considerable, the cultural impact is also notable.

According to Parsi beliefs, vultures serve as intermediaries between earth and sky. The dead body is placed on a Tower of Silence where vultures, by consuming the body, liberate the soul. The 82,000 Parsi Indians, deprived of their celestial emissaries, have been obliged to drop these ancient customs, since now bodies take six months to disappear.

Same situation prevails in the mountainous country, Tibet which also practices sky burials.

Catastrophic Results

A brief résumé of the situation shows the extent of the catastrophe:

The most rapid decline in history of such a large population of any scavenger.

An increase in the number of wild dogs, vectors of serious transmissible diseases, such as rabies, anthrax, and plague.

The danger of a serious epidemic; anthrax, for example, has been used in biological weapons.

30,000 deaths from rabies annually; 70% are children under the age of 15.

A cultural community highly dependent on vultures, also in decline.

The economic cost to India: 34 billion US dollars every year.

References:

http://www.iucnredlist.org/ Houston, 1985

Indian statistics, 2001

ILC 2003, projection based on Animal Husbandry Statistics, Government of India.

Birds of prey of the Indian subcontinent, Rishad Naoroji, 2007, Om Books international

Bombay Natural History Society

13.

The Bad Press

And A Thankless Task

As soon as you spot some vultures, you think of them as disgusting, ugly, greedy creatures who are after your flesh. When Charles Darwin went across the Atlantic on HMS Beagle in 1832, he saw the Turkey Vultures. He described them as : "….. disgusting birds with bald scarlet heads formed to revel in putridity." They have also been associated with Disney and are personified as goofy, dumb characters.

British naturalists in colonial India considered them to be among the ugliest birds, and their habit of feeding on faeces was particularly despised.

They have an undeservedly bad reputation. Because we associate carrion with disease, people believed that vultures spread diseases. But in fact, we now know that the opposite is true. Their powerfully

> Both the hummingbird and the vulture fly over our nation's deserts. All vultures see is rotting meat, because that is what they look for. They thrive on that diet. But hummingbirds ignore the smelly flesh of dead animals. Instead, they look for the colorful blossoms of desert plants. The vultures live on what was. They live on the past. They fill themselves with what is dead and gone. But hummingbirds live on what is. They seek new life.
> ~ Malayan Proverb

corrosive stomach acids allow them to safely digest carrion that would be lethal to other scavengers, wiping out bacteria that can cause diseases like botulism and anthrax. They are the purgers of death and disease.

They are the hardiest of God's creations and have been called nature's own disposal squads. Carcasses - rotting ones at that - are a vulture's typical diet and its scavenging habits are an important link in checking and containing  the spread of infectious diseases among animals and human beings.

Poets and writers have written eloquently on parrots, woodpeckers, hornbills, cuckoos and bulbuls, but few have spared a thought for the vulture. Even if the bird does find notice it is usually for the wrong reasons.

Whenever there are occurrences of cattle epidemics causing large-scale deaths or natural calamities like floods and droughts,

I want to conclude this post by briefly relating my personal experiences with vultures as an intern in 2010 at The World Bird Sanctuary. During my time at the sanctuary, I got to work up close with Black Vultures, Egyptian Vultures, Hooded Vultures, King Vultures and Turkey Vultures. One of the things I remember most about the vultures is that they liked to try to nip my arms and hands a lot. The Hooded Vultures in particular were fond of "accidentally" biting my hand instead of the food in my glove. They were really cool birds to work with though and I remember them fondly. Several times I had the chance to help train a Hooded Vulture and enjoyed it. I also laughed at the antics of the Turkey Vultures when they were getting excited about feeding time. Sure, they may not be the prettiest birds but they have unique personalities and are fun to watch. Vultures, nature's clean-up crew!

~ Josh

nature assigns the vulture with the job of cleansing the earth of putrid carcasses thus speedily preventing deadly germs from spreading.

Residents in Pithauli, a Nepalese village of more than 6,000 people, tell how villagers carried out special "purification" rites when vultures perched on the roofs of their homes.

When an old villager died a few days after a vulture had alighted on his house, it was widely believed to have resulted from his failure to perform the proper ritual.

This is because the job nature

"Why should I feel bad? We're part of nature's original recycling program!"

has assigned to them is unappealing. And the manner in which these fabulous birds of prey are portrayed in movies, TV shows and other media is less than flattering.

On Sept. 5 — the first annual International Vulture Awareness Day — zoos and bird societies around the globe will sponsor educational tours and flight demonstrations to get the word out about the plight of the vultures. Unlike blue whales, polar bears and other beloved species in danger of extinction, it may be harder to rally folks to save these prickly feathered birds with bumpy, bald heads, portly physiques and a tendency to be knee-deep in rotting flesh. "People look at vultures and see an ugly bird," Aversa says. "We will try to change attitudes and raise awareness of these scavengers in the ecosystem."

And vultures — despite their morbid reputation — will certainly respond warmly to human assistance. As the vulture barbershop quartet sings to Mowgli in Disney's The Jungle Book, "We're your friends to the bitter ends ... Who's always eager to extend a friendly claw?"

~ A Restaurant for Vultures. Literally - TIME Article

They are believed to be harbingers of death and associated with carcasses. Being great big ugly birds, they naturally do not attract our attention, like the beautifully iridescent humming bird for instance.

In the animal kingdom it's ironic that we glorify predators, like the lion, while we vilify scavengers, like the vulture, that clean up the mess left behind. Even the great Benjamin Franklin was unable to fight this prejudice in his preference of the turkey over the eagle (a predator) as a national symbol. If you encounter a lion on the savannah, it will kill you. If you run across a vulture in the process of cleaning up the carnage caused by the lion, it will save you from a possible epidemic.

Unlike lions and other large predators, vultures don't need to kill to survive. They serve a useful purpose in areas with poor or non-existent sanitation. This, however, does not make them popular and it is doubtful that any major league sports teams would ever choose a vulture as a mascot.

References:

Destroying the Disposers of Death: Will India Rescue its few Remaining Vultures? Aatish Bhatia

Nepal's vulture "restaurants" for endangered birds, Reuters

Vultures – An Essential Part of The Real Estate Ecosystem, propertyradar.com

Clipping The Wings Of The Vulture, Gyan Marwah

14.

Vultures

No Substitute

Recent studies have shown that in the areas where there are no vultures, carcasses taken upto 3-4 times longer to decompose. This has huge ramifications for spread of the diseases.

Also, vultures work round the year where as many other scavengers work seasonally. In Europe for example, ravens congregate in large flocks only in winter and thus they fail to provide ecosystem services year round.

As birds vultures can travel using soaring flight with low energy requirements and are far more efficient at exploiting this food resource than any mammalian carnivore.

Many small scavengers need to have open wounds on carcasses to get access to the meat. Vultures are capable of ripping open their carcasses. Large predators leave their kills with open wounds. Game that dies of another cause like old age, disease or parasites does not have open wounds. So the presence of large predators is needed.

When vultures surround you, try not to die.
~ *Proverb*

Vultures have the best feeding strategy as far as containment of diseases is concerned. Other scavengers may end up spreading diseases. Ravens for example do not actually feed at the carcass. They fill their craw with meat, hide it away and come back for more meat. This can spread the bacteria to a larger geographical area.

The great ornithologist, Dr. Salim Ali in The Book of Indian Birds described vultures as God's own incinerators, which cannot be replaced by even the most sophisticated ones which man may invent.

How important the vulture is to the eco-system is demonstrated by the fact they consume 70% of all meat in the Masai Mara in Africa. If they die, out there is no other animal that can consume that much amount of meat. On an aesthetic and health point of view alone, the spectacle of the Wildebeest migration would be somewhat spoilt should the savannah be littered with hundreds or

Decline in vulture population has led to increased availability of human carcasses to predators like leopards, thus turning them into man-eaters.

Man-eating leopards are a small percent of all leopards, but have undeniably been a menace in some areas; one leopard in India killed over 200 people. Jim Corbett was noted to have stated that unlike tigers, which usually became man-eaters because of infirmity, leopards more commonly did so after scavenging on human corpses; in the area that Corbett knew well, dead people are usually cremated completely, but when there is a bad disease epidemic, the death rate outruns the supply of cremation pyre wood and people burn the body a little and throw it over the edge of the burning ghat. In Asia, man-eating leopards usually attack at night, and have been reported to break down doors and thatched roofs in order to reach human prey. Attacks in Africa are reported less often, though there have been occasions where attacks occurred in daylight. Both Corbett and Kenneth Anderson have written that hunting the man eating panther presented more challenges than any other animal.

thousands of carcasses. Tourists' travelling around national game parks wearing masks to prevent them from enduring the stench of rotting carcasses or ingesting airborne diseases is not an appealing vision.

The vulture-governed cleaning service protects the health of humans, domesticated animals, and wildlife because the abundance of other scavengers, some of which are well-known disease reservoirs, increases substantially at carcasses without vultures.

Scavenging of carcasses by vultures promotes the flow of energy through food webs, and vultures have been shown to facilitate African predators, such as lions and hyenas, in locating food resources.

As carrion specialists, the absence of vultures from carcasses may affect the community composition of scavengers at carcasses, which could alter scavenging rates for individual species. Diseases such as rabies and bubonic plague, for which dogs and rats respectively are the primary reservoirs, may increase as a consequence of vulture declines.

In India, rising cases of anthrax infection due to handling infected carcasses or consuming poorly cooked meat of infected livestock are believed to be linked to the precipitous decline of vultures.

African white-backed vulture
Is the most common scavenger in Masai Mara. The pirannas of the savannas, these vultures can eat over 1 kg (2 lbs) of meat in just two minutes and feed in huge groups, sometimes of over 100 individuals.

In Kenya, in the absence of vultures, carcass decomposition time nearly tripled, and both the number of scavenging mammals and the time they spent at carcasses increased threefold. Further, there was a nearly threefold increase in the number of contacts between mammalian scavengers at carcasses without vultures, suggesting that the demise of vultures could facilitate disease transmission at carcasses.

In African savannas, species most likely to increase in abundance in the absence of vultures are hyenas and jackals. This can heavily impact the delicate web of life there. Hyenas and jackals host a number of pathogens that infect a wide range of other wild and domesticated species (Alexander et al. 1994; Harrison et al. 2004).

Two major diseases that affect African carnivores, rabies and canine distemper, spread through direct contact between infected and susceptible individuals, and carnivores often interact closely at carcasses (Mills 1993; Roelke-Parker et al. 1996; Butler et al. 2004).

Bangladesh, a region with substantial declines in vulture abundance, has seen a surge in crow population and dead crows have tested positive for the highly pathogenic influenza virus (H5) (Giasuddin et al. 2009).

The lack of vultures is something that should be at the forefront of conservation but all too often is hidden behind the public's desire for the cute & cuddly. We must not allow the attractive but environmentally more impotent of our species to relegate key species to the back pages. We must learn to value our vultures before we lose them.

References:
Government inaction, lack of funding worsen vulture crisis, especially in Africa, The Peregrine Fund

---

Don't play dead with a vulture. That's exactly what they want.
Kevin Nealon

Decline of the Vulture, http://www.glo-wild.com/

Sudarshan MK. Assessing burden of rabies in India. WHO sponsored national multi-centric rabies survey (May 2004). Assoc Prev Control Rabies India J 2004;6:44-

Society for Masheer Conservancy, 2008

BNHS, Société zoologique de Londre, 2007

15.

Vulture Restaurants

A Vulture Restaurant is a specific site where carcasses are provided as a source for vultures to feed from. They are unique eaters in that they only feed from the meat of dead animals. Their numbers have plummeted due to a decline in habitat and food supply, nest disturbances and collisions with power lines.

Several vulture restaurants have been set up in different parts of the world to attract vultures. The restaurants allow for a supplement to the bird's natural food supply. It allows them to feed on safe meat in an undisturbed area. The bones  of the carcass are often chipped to allow for maximum calcium and mineral availability.

Farmers have been encouraged to participate in the conservation effort by donating animals that have died of old age or other causes. It is an economical and hygienic way to dispose of their livestock carcasses. Volunteer veterinarians check to ensure the carcass is free of any toxins, then it can be placed at a protected vulture restaurant location. There you go, a la carte vulture style!

Restaurant should be an area of open field where the vultures can easily land and take off without interference. It is best placed out of sight of roads or human traffic so that the vultures can feed without disturbance. Placement far from powerlines is important to prevent collisions and electrocution. It should be about 50 m by 50 m and should be fenced to keep out jackals and other potential problem animals. If possible, the grass should be mown or burnt to keep it short as generally the vultures feel unsafe in tall grass. The placement of a nearby dead tree for them to perch in prior to coming down makes them feel safer. A small shallow pan with water is often appreciated by

'MY FOOD IS FRESHLY MADE, IT DOESN'T STINK, THERE ARE NO MAGGOTS ON IT, IT'S NOT EVEN A BIT MOULDY - AND YOU DARE TO CALL THIS A 3-STARS-RESTAURANT??!'

the vultures and this may also help keep them out of the drinking troughs placed on the farm for domestic livestock.

Restaurant hygiene should be practiced to prevent the site from becoming unsightly and possibly offensive to less vulture-friendly neighbours.

> *A vulture on board; bald, red, queer-shaped head, featherless red places here and there on his body, intense great black eyes set in featherless rims of inflamed flesh; dissipated look; a business-like style, a selfish, conscienceless, murderous aspect--the very look of a professional assassin, and yet a bird which does no murder. What was the use of getting him up in that tragic style for so innocent a trade as his? For this one isn't the sort that wars upon the living, his diet is offal--and the more out of date it is the better he likes it. Nature should give him a suit of rusty black; then he would be all right, for he would look like an undertaker and would harmonize with his business; whereas the way he is now he is horribly out of true.*
>
> *~ Mark Twain, Following the Equator*

When placing carcasses at a vulture restaurant it is important to ensure that they have not been treated with poisons (e.g. barbiturates to euthanize them) or with harmful veterinary drugs.

A vulture restaurant should only be started in areas where vultures are indeed seen from time to time. Otherwise the carcasses will just lie about the field, decomposing and attracting flies.

References:

Baker, EC Stuart (1928). The Fauna of British India. Birds. Volume 5 (2 ed.). London: Taylor and Francis. pp. 22–24.

Vulture Restaurants, Audrey, http://www.travelfootprints.ca/

Endangered Wildlife Trust, Vulture Restaurants, Steven Piper,

16.

Vulture Restaurants In India

India Throws Vultures A Bone - Literally.

After the disappearance of vultures from Indian skies, there has been attempt to save the remain few hundred by opening 'restaurants' for them. Across the country, several such sites have been opened. On the one hand meat, their food, is being exported and on the other, this show of solidarity is being made.

Phansad Wildlife Sanctuary

Deep in the wildlife sanctuary, a swath of grasslands opens onto a clearing so dry the ground looks covered in yellow hay. In the middle of the clearing, leftover cow teeth, hooves and bones are strewn about.

In an effort to save the scavengers from extinction, the state of Maharashtra has embarked on a project to create a safe space where the birds can eat and mingle.

The restaurant serves vulture delicacies: cow, water buffalo and bullock carcasses. Forest officials secure the carcasses from nearby villages.

"Vultures are a very important part of nature," says Raju Kasambe, who runs a bird conservation project for the Bombay Natural History Society. "They are nature's own cleaner. When an animal or cattle is dead in the forest there is no body to clean it except for vultures."

Without the scavengers, the slowly decaying carcasses can spread odor and even diseases in a village, Kasambe says. Stray dogs and smaller scavenger birds like house crows and black kites have become more common. These birds are problematic, he adds, because they feed on other birds'

It's not quite dead. I'd say three more circlings should do it.

nests and decrease environmental biodiversity. The dogs can bite people and spread diseases.

To prevent other animals from snacking on the vultures' food, officials have built a chain-link fence around the 2-acre plot. There are platforms on which carcasses are served and some wooden logs where the birds can perch.

The success of the restaurant will depend on the forest officials' ability to secure enough food for the vultures. "In the past, villagers skinned dead animals for their hides and then left the carcass in the field for the scavengers", says one forest official. "These days, villagers take their old animals to slaughterhouses, thus leaving nothing for the poor vultures", he adds.

In order to encourage the villagers to let their animals die naturally and then give them to the sanctuary, the forest department is paying them more than the butchers.

They have a budget of Rs. 50,000 ($900) for the year to run the establishment.

Another way to save the birds is through artificial breeding, which the Bombay Natural History Society conducts at breeding centers in the Indian states of Haryana, West Bengal and Assam. After a vulture lays an egg, the conservationists remove the egg and incubate it artificially. This program has been successful, and 18 vultures are now ready to be released into the wild.

Officials acknowledge that this project has produced a small number of vultures given the hundreds of thousands that have died off.

To celebrate the project's success and to create awareness about the important role of the scavengers in the food chain and ecology, the department held a day-long vulture festival on April 12, 2011 at the sanctuary.

Shrushtidnyan, an NGO has planned forest trails and bird watching, wildlife photography, film screenings, poster and photo exhibitions, slide shows, tattoo printing, drawing competition, mask painting competition, games and activities as part of the festival whose theme is 'Save Vultures - Save Nature'.

The wildlife wing of the forest department plans to set up more such vulture restaurants in Thane, Nagpur, Nashik, Raigad and Gadchiroli districts. While Dr Ajay Poharkar, raptor scientist and secretary of the National Association for Welfare of Animals and Research, is already running a vulture restaurant in Nimgaon, in Gadchiroli, three such restaurants exist in Punjab.

The three sites in Punjab are all near fresh water, so the birds can bathe themselves after their messy meals.

Ref:
Hanna Ingber, January 3, 2011
Falguni Banerjee, TNN April 9, 2012

17.

Vulture Restaurants

Cambodian Experience

Vulture populations in Southeast Asia are primarily threatened by the declining number of large herbivores in the region.

Vulture conservation efforts in Cambodia are the result of a number of activities promoted by the Cambodia Vulture Conservation (WCS) Project. For instance, vulture nests are protected by local community members who are paid a small fee for their support. This ensures that vulture nesting success is greatly improved and also benefits local community members who often have few other sources of income during the dry season, which coincides with the vulture breeding season. Vulture food sources are supplemented by 'vulture restaurants,' feeding stations that also give visitors the opportunity to see these huge birds up close.

This project is a partnership of different government agencies and conservation organisations led by WCS and also includes the Forestry Administration of the Ministry of Agriculture, Fisheries and Forestry, the General Department of Administration for Nature Conservation and Protection of the Ministry of Environment, BirdLife International in Indochina, Worldwide Fund for Nature, Angkor Centre for Conservation of Biodiversity (ACCB) and Conservation International.

Researchers report that 296 birds of three species have been found at multiple sites across the Northern and Eastern Plains of Cambodia. This count means that Cambodia is home to the only stable population of vultures in Asia. All three of Cambodia's vulture species are listed as "Critically Endangered" by the World Conservation Union (IUCN).

The census success follows a record breeding season for vultures in Cambodia. This year, a total of 36 vulture chicks fledged from colonies across the north and east of the country, an increase from last year's total of 19 chicks

Vulture Restaurant Sites

Currently, there are six permanent vulture restaurant sites in the north and northeastern part of the country, and upper Mekong River region.

In these restaurants, tourists come to watch vultures from a 'hide'. The groups arrive at the hide before dawn in order to witness the feeding spectacle of up to 70 birds on a single carcass as the sun comes up.

References:

Vulture Numbers on the Increase, WCS

Increase in Cambodia's Vultures Gives Hope to Imperiled Scavengers, Wildlife Conservation Society, Cambodia

18.

Nepal

'Eateries' For Endangered Birds

This is one restaurant you may visit but not order anything for yourself. And if you want to see the patrons having a meal, do so discreetly lest you disturb them.

In the village of Pithauli, surrounded by ripening mustard fields, a woman hauls a cow carcass on a trolley, drops it in an open field, then runs and hides in a nearby hut as dozens of vultures swoop down.

In under half an hour, the carcass has been reduced to bones by the dun-colored birds, occasionally squabbling as they feed.

The site is one of a handful of vulture "restaurants" opened to save the birds, which help keep the environment clean by disposing of carrion, from extinction -- and at the same time help impoverished villages.

Two decades ago there were about 50,000 nesting pairs of the two vulture species in Nepal. Now, barely 500 pairs remain.

"If the present situation continues the vulture species will be extinct in ten years," said Hem Sagar Baral, chief of the Nepalese Ornithological Union.

"We may maintain certain minimum numbers but we'll never see the numbers we had 20 years ago."

Apart from lack of food, their steep decline is also blamed on the loss of habitat, with the kapok trees they use for nesting vanishing fast to meet demand from factories producing match sticks and plywood.

Five years ago, Bird Conservation Nepal came up with the idea of "restaurants" as places where the birds could feed on safe carcasses.

Pithauli, some 100 km (60 miles) southwest of the Nepali capital of Kathmandu, was the site of the first such feeding station, which now number six around the country. Incidently, this is also the first community-managed vulture feeding station (and vulture information centre) in the world, developed with funds from the United Nations Development Programme.

The number of nesting pairs there has grown to 46 compared with just 17 before the feeding site was opened five years ago, says Dhan Bahadur Chaudhary, who coordinates the project.

In addition, despite the vulture's positive depiction in Hindu scriptures as fighting to free Sita, wife of the God-king Rama from the clutches of a demon, the birds are widely reviled as ugly and the harbingers of bad luck.

Jatayu Restaurant, Chitwan National Park

Authorities have set up a vulture breeding centre in the Chitwan National Park in the neighboring jungle resort of Kasara, where 60 birds, captured in the wild, are being raised. Ultimately, they plan to release chicks into the wild.

The vulture restaurant has become a tourist attraction in the poverty-stricken village, and admission fees from visitors -- who last year numbered some 2,000 -- help support it.

This provides an economic and practical way of disposing of dead cattle. Scientists are able to study the biology and ecology of these threatened species. Very importantly, these help raise public awareness on vulture conservation and to raise funds.

Authorities buy old and sick cattle from the villagers and these animals are kept on a farm in a community-run forest and offered to the birds when they die naturally since killing a cow is a criminal offence in deeply Hindu Nepal.

Ghachowk

The Ghachowk vulture restaurant, established during 2010, is located in a river valley in the foothills of the Himalayas about 15 km northeast of Pokhara. The restaurant is about 20-minute walk down into the gorge.

Along the way vultures can be seen and photographed in flight and perching on nearby low cliffs. At the restaurant, observers sit in a well constructed hide that holds up to 10 people (suggested donation $3), approximately 25 meters from where the carcasses are placed. The vultures perch in the nearby trees for several hours or sit along the nearby river before coming to feed on the carcass.

The restaurant is operated under the auspices of Bird Conservation Nepal and the Royal Society for the Protection of Birds (RSPB).

Gaindahwa Lake

This restaurant is located approximately 15 km north of the town of Lumbini (the birth place of Buddha) in the terai of west-central Nepal.

At this site an abundance of juvenile and subadult Himalayan Griffons are found.

There are three other vulture restaurants; two, Lalmatiya and Syalapani, are in Dang District, roughly 125 km west of the restaurant at Gaindahwa Lake, whilst the third, in the far south-west of Nepal, lies within the Samaiji Community Forest in Kailali

District. More details about these sites can be found in the Bird Conservation Nepal (2009) brochure, Jatayu Restaurant.

Ref:

Ajay Jain, 15 March 2010

Gopal Sharma Pithauli, Nepal Tue Feb 7, 2012

Elaine Lies and Paul Casciato (Reuters)

Visiting A Restaurants

The admission fee to each of the six vulture restaurants in Nepal is approximately $3. Guides have the best knowledge of when a carcass becomes available at a particular restaurant because they are in frequent cell-phone contact with restaurant coordinators. Vultures readily come down to feed if a carcass has not been provided for four days or more. On the other hand, if carcasses have been recently available the vultures might take several hours to descend from roosting trees. Groups of up to six people are ideal since noise and movement while getting into the wooden hides can be easily minimised, hence the vultures will come to the carcass to feed sooner. However, if the vultures are shy eaters when you visit, it is still possible to get wonderful photos of them perched and in flight.

Rural people who once disliked vultures are beginning to appreciate them because they bring money into their villages. It is hoped that the 'vulture safe zones' that surround the feeding sites are significantly enlarged and vulture nesting colonies are actively protected. With educational outreach from NGOs such as Bird Conservation Nepal and Himalayan Nature, both rural and urban people now realise the health benefits for humans that these birds deliver—a large carcass can be consumed in less than an hour by a flock of hungry vultures. In Nepal, dead animals and refuse are often dumped into rivers, and this practice can quickly spread disease to people living downstream (Baral 2009).

19

South Africa

New Vulture Restaurants

South African vultures are facing ever-increasing threats. Of the nine vulture species that occur in South Africa, seven are listed in the South African Red Data List, ranging from Threatened to Critically Endangered. The main cause of the demise of this important raptor group is a declining food source, although other issues such as loss of foraging areas, electrocution on electricity pylons, and inadvertent poisoning also have a strong influence on their numbers.

BirdLife South Africa, a voluntary organization, has recently been involved in developing a number of infrastructure development projects including the establishment of a vulture restaurant and hide, 20 km south of Phalaborwa.

The purpose of this new viewing hide is threefold. Its main purpose is to provide exceptional, close-up views of these magnificent birds, but more importantly it will serve as an educational facility highlighting the plight of vulture populations in southern Africa which are in a drastic state of decline.

BirdLife South Africa plans to bring school groups to the hide to show them the importance of vultures in the ecology as well as to dispel the myths surrounding the birds.

Carcasses are normally only put down at the weekends, ensuring that the birds do not become dependent on the additional food source. This vulture restaurant is one of just a few that are located within the reserve and hyaena and other carnivores frequent the carcasses.

The visitor book also reveals that it is not uncommon to find yourself surrounded by more than 150 vultures during feeding time.

Limpopo Province

The Limpopo Province falls within the distribution range of most of these species, with the exception of the Bearded Vulture. Furthermore, one of the most active vulture restaurants in the country can be found less than 20km from the centre of Polokwane on the Mockford farm. This vulture restaurant regularly attracts species such as the Cape, White-backed, Hooded and Lappet-faced Vultures.

25 Vultures To Be Fitted With Tracking Devices

Two different prominent vulture restaurants have been identified as capture sites in the Limpopo Province where 25 vultures will be captured and fitted with GSM tracking devices. The tracking devices will allow the investigators to see how vulture restaurants influence the movements of vultures. This will be done by analysing the movement of vultures over a one year period.

Lesotho

Lesotho is small country landlocked within South Africa. From the highway, the vulture restaurant is visible in the distance. Often one can see several dark objects on animal carcasses lying there.

The Bearded Vulture mainly inhabits mountainous areas. A drastic decline in the numbers has resulted in a population that is limited to the highlands of Lesotho and the adjacent mountains. These fascinating creatures can be viewed at the Golden Gate National Park vulture restaurant, located in the Drakensberg Mountains of South Africa. The vulture restaurants provide excellent photographic opportunities and a unique experience for tourists.

The African White-backed Vulture is widespread in southern Africa, especially Botswana, the eastern and northern areas of Namibia and parts of Zimbabwe. Although widespread, they have declined rapidly in certain parts of their range. Recent research has shown that vultures are highly mobile and can cover several 100 kilometres in a day in search of food. This makes the implementation of effective conservation measures a daunting task which conservationists and researchers propose is best approached from a regional perspective.

In Africa, conservationists are calling for a cross-border conservation effort as soon as possible, and it is hoped that the tracking research will provide information to assist this conservation work.

Kempenfeldt Vulture Restaurant

Kempenfeldt is a privately owned farm in the Dundee district of Northern Natal and it is hosting a well know vulture feeding site. There is a wide range of fauna and flora. Topography drops from tall, dry grassveld to valley Bushveld with no frost. In the valley is a waterfall ensuring a continuous flow of fresh water.

It has beautiful views into the Wasbank Valley and big Coral and Bottle Brush trees host more than 160 species of birds.

Every September there is a National Vulture Awareness Day. Various species are observed and counted by KZN Wildlife. In 2009, 63 Cape Vultures and 425 Whitebacked Vultures were documented.

School groups are part of an outreach and education program on the conservation of vultures in the Dundee district. Regular interest groups and visitors are accommodated at Kempenfeldt. The exhilaration of children faces are rewarding when they see vultures for the first time in there natural habitat.

Kempenfeldt Vulture Hide is one of the best in the province and South Africa.

The Drakensburg

The Drakensberg (derived from the Afrikaans "Dragon Mountains") is the name given to the eastern portion which encloses the central Southern African plateau. It reaches its greatest altitude in this region (2000 – 3000 m).

Vulture restaurants in this area are mostly operated by an organization called Bird of Prey Working Group AGM. They regularly make presentations on falcons, harriers, vultures etc. for the visiting tourists.

Vulture restaurants in this area are located mostly on farms where people leave out dead animals regularly at the same place for vultures to come down and eat.

References:

Giving vulture conservation wings in Limpopo, Wildlife Extra

Kempenfeldt Vulture Restaurant, vulturehide.co.za

Muti

Vultures are highly prized by African traditional healers, or Muti, as they believe vultures have the ability to foresee into the future, which is why they are sought after for lotto and gambling purposes. Muti believe that if you sniff the brain of a vulture or sleep with the skull under your pillow you will then dream of the correct lotto numbers or the name of the winning horse and thus win millions. Other uses include vulture feathers, which are believed to cure headaches, and vulture feet which are worn as lucky charms. Unfortunately, according to most traditional healers and muti-practitioners, there is no alternative. And, as the South African government recognises the use of traditional healers, any associated costs are met by medical aid which places even more pressure on the vulture species.

South Carolina

Restaurant For Birds Of Prey

An avian conservation center in South Carolina is working to help bolster the U.S. vulture population by providing animal carcasses to birds and allowing human visitors to watch them feed.

The vulture restaurant will feature carrion served "buffet-style" at the Center for Birds of Prey in Awendaw, South Carolina, according to the center's website. It aims to promote vulture conservation by teaching visitors about the value of the scavenging birds.

"Mostly, it's an education tool for us," Center education director Stephen Schabel says, "It'd be great to see a societal change where every community has a vulture restaurant to get rid of roadkill."

Some vultures in the U.S. are harmed by eating carcasses in poisoned landfills, while others fall prey to vehicles while feeding on roadkills.

Ref:

CBS Charlotte reports.

© *2012 CBS Interactive Inc.*

Spain

Vulture Restaurants

Before the onset BSE (Bovine spongiform encephalopathy) many Spanish villages used traditional "muladares" to dump dead animals. This helped to sustain Spain's large vulture population. The arrival of BSE saw the introduction of new rules banning this practice and obliging farmers (and hunters) to clear up any dead animals as quickly as possible. Inevitably, this meant a sharp reduction in the availability of carrion and a threat to the continued existence of vultures.

Accordingly, "vulture restaurants" - fenced areas where carefully monitored carcasses (often horses or mules which are not vulnerable to BSE) - were created to provide these scavengers with a regular food supply. These feeding stations have since become the main food source for all avian scavengers.

This has doubtless helped them to maintain, even increase, their numbers. It's not all good news though. Evidently, their use has meant an increase in interspecies competition and a consequent decline in breeding success in some species. Similarly, the increase in crows opportunistically using the 'restaurants' has cause a sharp decrease in the breeding success of other bird species near these sites.

Furthermore, it's altered the habits of vultures who, rather than cruise the skies in search of food, are now more likely to loaf around near the more certain sources of food. There's also been a worryingly large increase in the levels of veterinary drugs in Spain's vultures. Presumably, this reflects the change in the origins of available carcasses and it's not yet clear what the long term impact of this might be.

Alcornocales

Whatever the pros and cons, these "restaurants" have provided easier and more predictable places to see vultures on the ground. Unfortunately, with few exceptions, the existence and exact location of these sites has not been widely publicised.

The "Birding map of the Alcornocales" – freely available at Natural Park Information offices – does shows two feeding stations; one at Montera del Torero and another below El Picacho.

"Take two carcasses and call me in the morning."

The watch point here is complete with signs and information (in English and Spanish) and looks across to the fenced area (to keep out Foxes, etc) where the carrion is left.

Unfortunately, the notice boards give no indication of when or how often food is distributed. Accordingly, whether you get to see vultures feeding is somewhat hit and miss. There's another restaurant not too far from the ruins of Acinipo.

Castellon Province

Since June 2000 a feeding site has been operational in the Villahcrmosa del Rio district in Castellon province.

Lying in the cast of the Iberian Peninsula, it is characterized by being at the junction of two great mountain ranges. As a result, there is a much-folded peak line of sedimentary rocks, of mostly calcareous material, with many cliffs and walls providing suitable Eurasian Griffon nesting sites.

Since the 1950s, there has been a progressive human exodus from the Spanish countryside to the towns. This has resulted in changes to the frequency and methods of carcass disposal in the countryside and has affected vultures in areas where they were dependent on humans for food. In the last five decades, it has affected all scavenging birds.

The unpredictable availability of the vultures' food has influenced various aspects of their biology and ecology including diet, colonial behaviour, breeding biology, distribution, migration and habitat use.

In this restaurant, the feeding area is fenced, but insider the fenced area there is also an observatory. Carcasses are brought to the feeding place in a four-wheel-drive vehicle. All the carrion originates from 6-8 local livestock operations, within 15 km of the restaurant.

Currently, four web cams are installed at the feeding place and the images arc available on the Internet.

Ref:

John Cantelo

Excm. Ayuntamiento de Villahermosa

22

Armenia

Vulture Restaurants - Serving and Saving Vultures

Vultures are keystone species that perform a vital ecosystem service by disposing of carrion. In Armenia, an 'Important Bird Area' (IBA) Caretaker is working with a network of local people to make livestock carcasses available for Cinereous Vulture, reviving a traditional disposal practice that is benefiting both farmers and the region's rarest raptors.

Armenia's Cinereous Vulture population fell to just six pairs in 2003. The decline is thought be linked to shortages of food.

Following the demise of Soviet infrastructure, there was an upsurge in the over-harvesting and illegal killing of wild and other mammals. This, coupled with changes in animal husbandry that resulted in huge

"Honestly, the water hole is back that way... Why would I lie?"

reductions in livestock, has dramatically reduced the amount of available carrion.

In addition, traditional methods of above-ground disposal of livestock carcasses and other waste are no longer commonly practiced. Vultures provide a crucial ecosystem service through the disposal of animal remains and their decline can have dramatic ecological and socio-economic consequences.

One response has been to establish feeding places for vultures or 'vulture restaurants', where the carcasses and waste products of animals from farms are put out for vultures.

Vardges Gharakhanyan, a local Caretaker at the Noravank IBA, is working with the priest of the Noravank monastery to establish a vulture feeding place in the IBA. By mobilising local community members, they are trying to make sure that all animal waste is saved and made available for vultures.

Pick-up of vulture food is arranged at weekends to allow disposal of all animal waste that accumulates over the week. Artificial feeding of vultures also has educational benefits and may result in an increase in the number of tourists who visit the IBA to see these birds.

References:

Empowering the Grassroots—BirdLife, Participation, and Local Communities'
BirdLife International (2011) A 'Vulture Restaurant' in Armenia solves
conservation and sanitation problems.

23.

Human Beings

The Wingless Vultures

It has been said that humankind are not true carnivores like lions and wolves. Rather they are necrovores, eaters of dead rotting flesh like vultures

An "aged steak" is one that has been allowed to (for lack of a better term) rot. The muscle fiber breaks down and the meat gets very tender. Ever see a chateaubriand (a French delicacy) before it's prepared to cook? Without a doubt it's rotting. Most of the meat we eat is rotten, it is just a question of degrees.

"Just bring us something dead."

Paul Watson, a Canadian environmentalist, (who founded the Sea Shepherd Conservation Society and known for the show 'Whale Wars') explains this.

"Humans do not eat like carnivores. Carnivores bring down living prey and eat it raw and most predators target the soft organs leaving much of the muscle for scavengers."

"Humans eat dead flesh and rarely eat the organs, preferring the muscle tissue. Most of the beef that people eat has been dead for months and in many cases years. The meat is disguised with bleach and dyes in many cases to hide the decay and the fact the the flesh is putrid. We are closer in our eating habits to vultures and jackals than wolves and lions."

"Technically speaking, humans are not carnivorous hominids. Humans fall into the necrovore category which means the eating of

---

Just like a small bird, immediately he can fly in the sky. And although we are very intelligent, if I want and if you want to fly in the sky, no you cannot. Although he's supposed to be very intelligent, a scientist, but he cannot fly. But a small bird will immediately fly. That is his prabhavah. You must have to admit that this is his special power. Similarly, a vulture, he goes four miles up and his eyes are very small. But from the four miles away he will find out where there is a dead body, immediately swoop down. And we have got much bigger eyes. But we cannot see even ... This spectacle required. You cannot see even one feet. So this is his prabhavah, influence.

A vulture, a nasty bird, still it has got so much influence that you cannot compete with him. So you'll find in every creature, every living entity, a special prerogative than the others.

Just like the hog. The hog can eat stool very nicely, very nicely. But although we say that everything is food, we can eat... Then you eat the stool? You cannot eat. He has got the influence that he can eat the stool very nicely.

Therefore we should not consider that all living entities are of the same status. They have different status. You cannot say because the other living entity is eating something abominable, therefore I can also eat, it is eatable. No, you cannot do that. If you eat, you will be diseased. Therefore, it is called, "one man's food is another man's poison." Prabhavas ca. Nobody can eat everything. Only his allotted food.

~ Srila Prabhupada (Lecture, Bhagavad-gita 13.4 -- Paris, August 12, 1973)

dead flesh. Humans do not kill their meat so much as they scavenge it. Even those of us who hunt do not kill and eat the hot living flesh of their victims. They wait for the meat to get cold and to begin the putrification process before consumption."

In the living entities lower than the human being, they follow the nature's way, their allotted food. Just like the tiger eats blood and flesh. If you offer him nice fruit, nice sweet rice, he'll not eat. Even the dog, they do not like the sweet rice or nice kachori and srngara. You'll see. They cannot eat. If they eat, they will fall diseased. In Bengal it is said, kukkure pete ghi sayanaya. Too much fatty things, if you give to the dog, he'll not be able to digest. So similarly, we are human beings, we have got special food. Special food.

Therefore Krsna says, Krsna's prasada will be taken, by whom? By the human being. Of course, it can be offered to any living entitiy. Therefore, a devotee will take the remnants of foodstuff offered to Krsna. Therefore Krsna says patram puspam phalam toyam yo me bhaktya prayacchati [Bg. 9.26].

~ Srila Prabhupada (Lecture, Bhagavad-gita 13.4 -- Paris, August 12, 1973)

24.

The Wingless

Watching The Winged Ones

Author Tim Harris gets a rare opportunity to watch critically endangered vultures dine…

It's 5:30 in the morning and I'm sitting in a covered trench in pitch darkness. Beside me, my friend Neil crouches behind his enormous lens, waiting for the first indications of a new day. The odour of rotting flesh wafts through the screen in front of us, not too bad but enough to remind us that the previous day a cow's carcass was dumped on the ground a few metres away.

Time moves slowly and I'm constantly trying to find a more comfortable position. No padded seats here. In fact, no seats at all, and the log I'm sitting on was definitely not ergonomically designed. We speak not a word, however, since silence is all-important.

Just after 6:00 now, and the 'whoosh' of a very large bird passes directly overhead, followed by some flapping and an evil-sounding hiss. I risk parting the reedy screen a few centimetres and notice that the sky has lightened by a few degrees, revealing the silhouettes

of several vultures in the top of a tree. Much closer, several of these giants are already jostling with each other on the ground, just 30 metres away.

I've never had a problem watching others eat but this is very special. The vultures spent yesterday afternoon investigating how best to gain access to the deceased bovine's best joints. Clearly that is no longer an issue since the animal has been reduced to a pile of bones and offal.

As the sun comes up over this corner of dipterocarp forest on the northern plains of Cambodia, the diners' identities are revealed. Most are Indian White-backed Vultures but there are also a handful of Red-headed Vultures with their strangely perplexed expressions. The latter seem to spend most of their time standing around, doing very little, but they are clearly one step up in the pecking order.

Then there are the Slender-billed Vultures with their black, snake-like necks, perfect for going deep inside any dead animal. It is quickly clear that they always get what they want. The others back away when the Slender-bills hiss out a warning. Screams, hisses and the sound of wings flapping … this is the accompaniment to the end game as bones are stripped of their last morsels of flesh.

Apart from their love of carrion, these vultures are sadly united by one thing: their extreme rarity. The 60-odd birds we are watching represent a significant proportion of the world's population of each species. All are classified as Critically Endangered, and extinction is now a real threat. It was not always so but vulture populations have crashed catastrophically since the 1990s, down by as much as 99 percent. Those populations that remain are now disjointed.

Visiting birders and photographers pay for the privilege of witnessing the vultures and the cash goes into the hands of the villagers who provide the carrion. To be fed and guided by local villagers is an inspirational experience.

Dining with vultures in Siem Pang

In July I was fortunate enough to spend a week in Siem Pang, northern Cambodia, with Jonathan Eames, Programme Manager at BirdLife in Indochina. For me, it was an opportunity to look at the tourism potential for Siem Pang and in particular the potential for birding tourism.

For all of us however there was another reason for making the long trek up to Siem Pang – the chance to attend one of BirdLife's monthly vulture restaurants. This area of northern Cambodia is one of the very few places left in South-East Asia where it is possible to see vultures in any numbers. With the exception of Burma vultures have all but disappeared from the countries of mainland South-East Asia.

The journey to Siem Pang was an adventure in itself involving a full day's drive from Phnom Penh to Stung Treng and then a 5-hour cruise by motorised canoe up the Stung Kong, a tributary of the Mekong, to Siem Pang. The river was teeming with birdlife.

Staying at the wooden stilted house that houses the BirdLife office at Siem Pang we explored the dry deciduous and semi-evergreen forest, grasslands and seasonal freshwater pools known as trapeangs by motorcycle. This remote area of northern Cambodia is one of the remaining refuges for some of the world's rarest birds.

The birds we had really come to see however were vultures, and we weren't disappointed. BirdLife's monthly vulture restaurants provide a convenient means of monitoring vulture numbers while at the same time providing a good square meal for the local vulture population.

A bullock carcass was left in a forest clearing around twenty metres away from a camouflaged hide where we sat with scopes and bins at the ready. Small groups of vultures were already gathering in the trees around the clearing when we arrived at the hide early the next morning but the first visitor was a Golden Jackal that had already taken a few bites out of the rump of the bullock carcass.

We had been waiting for around two hours by the time the first brave vulture made a move and with heavy wing beats dropped down from the trees and hopped over to the carcass. This was the signal the others had been waiting for and within seconds the whole group of vultures noisily descended on the bullock.

Then it was a free-for-all as 30 plus Vultures bickered, squabbled and gorged themselves. Two hours later the bullock carcass had been reduced to a pile of skin and bones.

References:

Dining at the Vulture Restaurant, Tim Harris, bloomsburywildlife

Vietnam Birding, Birdlife Indochina

25.

International Vulture Awareness Day

Let's Abstain From Meat For A Day

Vultures enjoy their own unique holiday, International Vulture Awareness Day, which is celebrated on the first Saturday of each September. The holiday is a way to raise awareness about these unique birds, and hundreds of zoos, aviaries, nature preserves and bird refuges worldwide participate each year with fun and informational activities about vultures.

Prabhupada: Yes. We recommend the meat-eaters, who eat dogs as Korea, they're eating dogs, so you can eat also dog. But don't... You eat it after death. We don't say don't eat. You are so much fond of eating. All right. You eat. Because after the death, we have to give the body to some living entity. So generally, it is given to the vultures. So why to the vultures? Take the civilized men, who are as good as vultures. (laughter) The so-called civilized men. Yes. What is the difference between the vultures and these rascals? The vultures also enjoy a dead body. And they also kill, make it dead and enjoy. They're vultures.

Yogesvara: Sakuni.

Prabhupada: Yes. Sakuni, yes. They're vultures, and their civilization is vulture-eater. The animal-eaters, they're like jackals, vultures, dogs. They're similar to these animals, the animal-eaters. It is not human food. Here is human food. Here is civilized food, human food. Let them learn it.

Around the world vultures are under-appreciated and therefore under protected. Let us think about the tons of rotting, diseased flesh that vultures dispose of annually. Now imagine if humans had to do that same job. The cost alone would be astronomical! So let us join hands in showing some respect and compassion to the vulture on this day by abstaining from meat, just for one day.

We can survive on so many types of eatables but vultures can only survive on rotten meat. We offer a direct competition to vultures by consuming something which rightfully belongs to them.

References:

Vultures: Ecosystem Guardians

Wildlife Research & Conservation

26.

A Vulture Civilization

In June of 1974, at the Hare Krishna movement's rural community near Valencey, France, Śrīla Prabhupāda talks to a group of intimate disciples. He points out that modern civilization's hunger for meat and its extensive system of vicious and barbaric slaughtering facilities bring karmic reactions in the form of world wars, which Śrīla Prabhupāda refers to as "slaughterhouses for humankind."

Śrīla Prabhupāda: For meat-eaters, that is what the Vedic culture recommends: "Don't eat cows until after they have died a natural death. We don't say, "Don't eat." You are so very fond of eating cows. All right, you can eat them, because after their death we have to give them to somebody, some living entity. Generally, cow carcasses

> In the various species of life there are various facilities for material sense gratification. Different species are distinguished by differently formed senses, such as the genitals, nostrils, tongue, ears and eyes. Pigeons, for example, are given the facility for almost unlimited sex. Bears have an ample opportunity for sleeping. Tigers and lions exhibit the propensities for fighting and meat-eating, horses are distinguished by their legs for swift running, vultures and eagles have keen eyesight, and so on. The human being is distinguished by his large brain, which is meant for understanding God.
> ~ Srila Prabhupada (Srimad Bhagavatam 11.3.3)

are given to the vultures. But then, why only to the vultures? Why not to the modern "civilized" people, who are as good as vultures? [Laughter.]

These so-called civilized people—what is the difference between these rascals and vultures? The vultures also enjoy killing and then eating the dead body. "Make it dead and then enjoy"—people have become vultures. And their civilization is a vulture civilization. Animal-eaters— they're like jackals, vultures, dogs. Flesh is not proper food for human beings. Here in the Vedic culture is civilized food, human food: milk, fruit, vegetables, nuts,

grains. Let them learn it. Uncivilized rogues, vultures, rākṣasas [demons]—and they're leaders.

> As far as our senses are concerned, there are many animals, both beasts and birds, who are very expert in exercising their senses more keenly than human beings. For example, vultures or hawks can go very high in the sky, but can see a small body on the ground very clearly. This means that their eyesight is so keen that they can find an eatable corpse from a great distance. Certainly their eyesight is much keener than human beings', but this does not mean that their existence is more important than that of a human being. Similarly, dogs can smell many things from a far distance. Many fish can understand by the power of sound that an enemy is coming. All these examples are described in Srimad-Bhagavatam. If one's senses cannot help him attain the highest perfection of life, realization of the Supreme, they are all useless.
>
> ~ Srila Prabhupada (Srimad Bhagavatam 4.31.11)

Therefore I say that today the leaders are all fourth-class men. And that is why the whole world is in a chaotic condition. We require learned spiritual teachers—first-class men—to lead. If people will take our advice, then everything will be all right. What is the use of fourth-class men leading a confused and chaotic society?

If I speak so frankly, people will be very angry. But basically, their leaders are all fourth class. *Śva-vid-varāhostra-kharaih samstutah purusah paśuh* [*Śrīmad-Bhāgavatam 2.3.19*]: People are living just like animals—without regulative, spiritual principles—and from among

---

In which way you are advanced? The animals, the trees, they are far advanced than you in this matter. So far bodily necessities are concerned, you cannot compete with them. You are flying. So we can fly by airplane. Oh, the vulture can fly more than you. It is a vulture, and it flies many miles above, and it has got very sharp eyesight. The vulture is so up. The business is where there is a dead body. That's all. He is trying to find out, "Where is a dead body?" You see? It goes high, but the business is to find out a dead body. That's all. Similarly, our, this advancement of science, increasing the duration of life, increasing the sex power especially in these days ... As soon as there is lack of sex power, there is divorce suit. Yes. But you have seen the dogs and cats. How much sex power they have got! So begetting children, the hog can beget children, at least three dozen a year. What we can do? In three years it is hardly we can produce one child. And the hog will produce in three years at least thirty-six children.

So you cannot compete. Simply by competing with these things, animal life, that is not excellence of your life. Real excellence is that these animals, they cannot become Krsna conscious. That is the difference only. You can excel with all these lower animals, trees, birds, beasts and others, so many, only by awakening your Krsna consciousness. That is the only business. And if you lack in that matter Krsna consciousness, then the other animals, lower animals, they are far, far advanced. They are far, far advanced.

~ Srila Prabhupada (Lecture, Srimad-Bhagavatam 2.3.18-19 -- Los Angeles, June 13, 1972)

themselves they are electing the biggest animals. Anyone can do whatever he likes, whatever he thinks—no regulative principles.

But human life is meant for regulative principles. We are insisting that our students follow regulative principles—no meat-eating, no illicit sex, no intoxication, no gambling—just to make them real human beings. Without regulative principles it is animal life. Animal life.

In the human form of life, after passing through millions of lives in the plant and animal species, the spirit soul gets the chance to take up the yoga system—and yoga means strict regulative principles. *Indriya-samyamah*—controlling the senses. That is the real yoga system. But today most people, though they may say they are practicing yoga, are misusing it. Just like the animals, they cannot control their senses. As human beings, they have higher intelligence; they should learn how to control the senses. This is human life. *Na yat-karna-pathopetah:* One who has not heard the message of Krishna, the Supreme Personality of Godhead—even for a moment—he's an animal. The general mass of people, unless they are trained systematically for a higher standard of life in spiritual values, are no better than animals. They are on the level of dogs, hogs, camels, and asses.

27

Say No To Eating Meat

Humans Are Not Physically Created To Eat Meat

Although some historians and anthropologists say that man is historically omnivorous, our anatomical equipments, teeth, jaws, and digestive system favor a fleshless diet. The American Dietetic Association notes that "most of mankind for most of human history has lived on vegetarian or near-vegetarian diets."

And much of the world still lives that way. Even in most industrialized countries, the love affair with meat is less than a hundred years old. It started with the refrigerator car and the twentieth-century consumer society. Without the refrigeration technology, human society would have to go hunting everyday to enjoy a meat based diet. Our addiction to meat squarely depends on widespread availability of refrigeration technology. Of course meat preservation techniques always existed but never on the industrial scale.

But even with the twentieth century, man's body hasn't adapted to eating meat. The prominent Swedish scientist Karl von Linne states, "Man's structure, external and internal, compared with that of the other animals, shows that fruit and succulent vegetables constitute his natural food."

The table below compares the anatomy of man with that of carnivorous and herbivorous animals.

When you look at the comparison between herbivores and humans, we compare much more closely to herbivores than meat eating animals. Humans are clearly not designed to ingest and digest meat.

Meat-eaters: have claws
Herbivores: no claws
Humans: no claws

Meat-eaters: have no skin pores and perspire through the tongue
Herbivores: perspire through skin pores
Humans: perspire through skin pores

Meat-eaters: have sharp front teeth for tearing, with no flat molar teeth for grinding
Herbivores: no sharp front teeth, but flat rear molars for grinding
Humans: no sharp front teeth, but flat rear molars for grinding

Meat-eaters: have intestinal tract that is only 3 times their body length so that rapidly decaying meat can pass through quickly
Herbivores: have intestinal tract 10-12 times their body length.
Humans: have intestinal tract 10-12 times their body length.

Meat-eaters: have strong hydrochloric acid in stomach to digest meat
Herbivores: have stomach acid that is 20 times weaker than that of a meat-eater
Humans: have stomach acid that is 20 times weaker than that of a meat-eater

Meat-eaters: salivary glands in mouth not needed to pre-digest grains and fruits.
Herbivores: well-developed salivary glands which are necessary to pre-digest grains and fruits

Someone taught me if you can't walk up to that animal and kill with your teeth then you're not supposed to eat it.
~ Anonymous

Humans: well-developed salivary glands, which are necessary to pre-digest grains and fruits

Meat-eaters: have acid saliva with no enzyme ptyalin to pre-digest grains

Herbivores: have alkaline saliva with ptyalin to pre-digest grains

Humans: have alkaline saliva with ptyalin to pre-digest grains

Based on a chart by A.D. Andrews, Fit Food for Men, (Chicago: American Hygiene Society, 1970)

Clearly if humans were meant to eat meat we wouldn't have so many crucial ingestive/digestive similarities with animals that are herbivores.

Many people ask, "If we weren't supposed to eat meat than why do we?" It is because we are conditioned to eat meat.

A popular statement that meat eaters say is; "In the wild, animals kill other animals for food. It's a part of nature." First of all, we are not in the wild. Secondly, we can easily live without eating meat and killing. We all would be healthier this way. Finally, as we have already seen, we weren't meant to eat meat. Meat putrefies within 4 hours after consumption and the remnants cling to the walls of the

Dr. Patel: This slaughterhouse, so abominable and so horrible. When I first came to Bombay from my village and I had to pass through that railway, that nasty butcher house. It was so horrible smelling and those vultures sitting on the...

Prabhupada: You were... Two thousand years ago, Christ, he was born in Jewish family, he was horrified by seeing animal sacrifices in the synagogue. Therefore his first commandment is, "Thou shall not kill." He was so horrified. Why he has given this commandment? He was so much horrified. What is this? Therefore he gave up the Jewish religion. He started his own. This is the history. And he first commanded, "Thou shall not kill."

~ Srila Prabhupada (Room Conversation -- December 31, 1976, Bombay)

intestines for 14-21 days. If a person is suffering from constipation the rotting meat can stay in the intestines for months or years. Furthermore, the saliva in humans is more alkaline, whereas in the case of flesh-eating or preying animals, it is clearly acidic. The alkaline saliva does not act properly on meat.

The final point that can be made on how we as humans were not meant to eat meat is this; all omnivorous and carnivorous animals eat their meat raw. When

If I had to kill to survive, I'd become a vegetarian

a lion kills an herbivore for food, it tears right into the stomach area to eat the organs that are filled with blood (nutrients). While eating the stomach, liver, intestine, etc., the lion laps the blood in the process of eating the dead animal's flesh. Even bears that are omnivores eat salmon raw. However, eating raw bloody meat disgust us as humans. This is why we must cook it and season it to buffer the taste of the flesh.

If a deer is burned in a forest fire a carnivorous animal will not eat its flesh. Even circus lions have to be feed raw meat so that they will not starve to death. If humans were truly meant to eat meat then we would eat all of our meat raw and bloody. The thought of eating such meat makes one's stomach turn. This is our point on

The point is humans do NOT need to eat meat at all. In fact, you will be much healthier by not eating meat. I am a vegetarian for over 30 years. Eat fresh fruits and vegetables, there are thousands of meat-less products and recipes to choose from. Why make your stomach a burial ground? Is your fridge a garden or a morgue?
~Steve, Baltimore.

how we as humans are conditioned to believe that animal flesh is good for us and that we were meant to consume it for survival and health purposes. If we are true carnivores or omnivores we would eat animal flesh raw and bloody. Cooking our meat and seasoning it with salt, ketchup, mayo, mustard or sauce disguise the awful taste of flesh. This is the only way we as humans would eat meat because we refuse to eat it raw and bloody like real carnivores.

Overall Advantages Of Vegetarianism

You can reap a lot of benefits by being a vegetarian and people have become more aware of the health benefits of being a vegetarian. Animal rights issues is only one of the reasons why people decide to go on a vegetarian diet. People are beginning to care more about the environment. However, the main reason why most people go on vegetarian diet is due to the health benefits.

Meat is not good for you as it clogs your thinking. This is especially true if you eat red meat; white meat has less fat compared to red meat. Excessive intake of fats

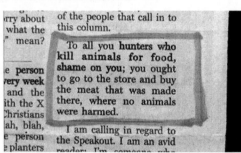

into your body can result in having a high level of cholesterol. If you think that not eating meat is going to make you look scrawny or unhealthy please think again. Just imagine that bulls, gorillas, elephants, rhinoceroses and so on are all vegetarians (herbivores) but look at how tough these animals are. They also have a longer life span compared to the carnivores (meat eating animals).

The Chinese believe that the chi or life force in your body is less when you consume meat and so do the Indians with their ancient yogic principles [their life force was called prana].

The great Tai Chi masters of China were adept at preserving their chi. Even though some of the masters were not vegetarians they still had a balanced diet. It has now been scientifically proven that a balanced vegetarian diet is better compared to a diet that is taken with meat.

> *Just like we are protecting cows. We cannot kill for the skin, but these asuras, they are killing thousands and thousands of cows for getting the skin, only for the skin. So if you are interested in the skin, if you are interested in the flesh, so at least wait for the time the animal will die. There is no doubt about it. So at least let him, let her die natural death. Why you should kill? You can take at that time the skin, the bone, the hoof. Whatever you like, you can take, the flesh. So in India there is a class. They are called camara. As soon as your animal is dead you give them information. They will come. They'll take the animal. They will get the skin for nothing. So they'll tan it and make shoes for selling. So they will get the raw materials free of charge. Tanning with oil and keeping it in the sunshine, the skin becomes soft and durable, and then you can prepare shoes. So there was no problem. And the bones you gather together and keep in a place. In due course of time it will become very good fertilization. And they can eat the flesh also. Only the cobbler class, the muci class, they eat this cow's flesh after taking the dead animal. So after killing, everyone eats, so why not wait for the natural death and eat it?*
>
> *But because they are asuras, raksasas, they do not wait for that. They want the fresh. What is that "fresh"? Unless you kill the animal, you cannot eat. So where is freshness? You have to kill him. You have to make it dead, so why not make it natural dead? And they have imagined something, this, that, vitamins, and so on, so on. This is asuras. So these asuras, they do not know that killing of an animal is sinful. You cannot... Just like we are sitting here, and if somebody comes and disturbs us and makes us obliged to leave this place, that is criminal. That is criminal. Similarly, a living entity has been ordained by the nature's law that he has to live in such and such body for a certain period. Living entity never dies. Na hanyate hanyamane sarire [Bg. 2.20]. So killing the body, he does not die, but because you disturb him, his duration of period to live in that body, you become sinful. You cannot disturb him.*
>
> *~ Srila Prabhupada (Bhagavad-gita 16.7 -- Hyderabad, December 15, 1976)*

There are a lot of misconceptions about being a vegetarian; protein is one of the main topics of debate as a lot of people think that you can only get protein from meat. Vegetarians get a lot of protein when they eat a variety of fruits, vegetables, grains and legumes. What vegetarians don't get is the excess protein of the traditional American diet. This type of diet leads to liver toxicity, kidney overload and mineral deficiency diseases.

A lot of people also think that a vegetarian diet is not a balanced diet. Vegetarian diets have a proportion of three macro nutrients which are complex carbohydrates, protein and fat. Vegetarian food sources (plants) tend to be higher sources of most micro nutrients. Another myth that needs to be clarified is the so-called lack of calcium among vegetarians. Many vegetables especially green leafy ones have a good supply of calcium. The truth is that vegetarians suffer less from osteoporosis (a deficiency of calcium that leads to weak bones).

Vegetarianism is our answer to complete health and wellness. The three issues to consider in regard to vegetarianism are: spiritual,

> *When we die, this material body composed of five elements -- earth, water, air, fire, and ether -- decomposes, and the gross materials return to the elements. Or, as the Christian Bible says, "Dust thou art, and unto dust thou shalt return." In some societies the body is burned, in others it is buried, and in others it is thrown to animals. In India, the Hindus burn the body, and thus the body is transformed into ashes. Ash is simply another form of earth. Christians bury the body, and after some time in the grave, the body eventually turns to dust, which again, like ash, is another form of earth. There are other societies -- like the Parsee community in India -- that neither burn nor bury the body but throw it to the vultures, and the vultures immediately come to eat the body, and then the body is eventually transformed into stool. So in any case, this beautiful body, which we are soaping and caring for so nicely, will eventually turn into either stool, ashes, or dust.*
>
> *~ Srila Prabhupada (Path of Perfection 8: Failure and Success in Yoga)*

mental and physical (nutritional). The spiritually aspiring person attempts to work on his/her self. The purpose of spiritual growth is to move away from the animal nature into the more human nature that God intended for us to have. Meat eating inhibits this.

The same science that attempts to ignore the existence of a force higher than man also proved that aggression levels are much higher in meat eaters than non-meat eaters! The animal instincts become more powerful every time you eat meat. Another spiritual aspect of being a meat eater is when one must question the necessity and method of killing animals. However, everyone has their own morals to which they must determine for themselves. Many spiritual people believe in auras. Kirilian photography shows us that a force field still remains around dead or amputated flesh. You adopt that animal aura when you eat it's dead flesh. Fruits and vegetables have a higher vibrational aura than animal products.

"You are what you eat", is a slogan that can be used to show the mental aspect of vegetarianism. When animals are slaughtered, fear and aggression enzymes are released into their muscle tissue. They remain in the meat until the consumer ingests the flesh and adapts the same emotions. Fruits and vegetables do not have emotions like animals; therefore, when they are picked they do not release any

> *Once a group of large hawks who were unable to find any prey attacked another, weaker hawk who was holding some meat. At that time, being in danger of his life, the hawk gave up his meat and experienced actual happiness.*
>
> *Incited by the modes of nature, birds become violent and kill other birds to eat them or to steal meat captured by them. Hawks, vultures and eagles are in this category. However, one should give up the envious propensity to commit violence against others and should take to Krsna consciousness, whereby one sees every living entity as equal to oneself. On this platform of actual happiness one does not envy anyone and thus sees no one as his enemy.*
>
> *~ Srila Prabhupada (Srimad Bhagavatam 11.9.2)*

emotional cells prior to digestion. The enzymes within fruits and vegetables supply the body with sufficient nutrients that will always uphold a healthy state of mind.

Fruits and vegetables are high in nutrients; the very thing the body needs to live a long disease and pain free life. The same cannot be said for meat. Nutritionally, the alkaline-based digestive system of humans will not properly break down substantial acid substances of meat.

Colon cancer is rampant! This is caused by the slow evacuation and putrefaction of meat in the colon. Lifelong vegetarians hardly ever suffer from such an illness. Many meat eaters believe that meat is the sole source of protein. However, the quality of this protein is so poor that little of it can ever be utilized by humans. This is due to its incomplete combination of amino acids [the building blocks of protein]. Studies show that the average American gets five times the amount of protein needed. It is a common medical

So the whole world, they are posing themselves as highly advanced in education -- science, philosophy, this, that, politics, so many things. But, their position is this body. Just like, an example, a vulture. A vulture rises very high. Seven miles, eight miles up. Wonderful, you cannot do that. And he has got wonderful eyes also. There are small eyes, vulture, it is so powerful that it can see from seven mile distance where there is a carcass, dead body. So he has got good qualification. He can rise very high, he can see from a distant place. Oh. But what is his object? A dead body, that's all. His perfection is to find out a carcass, dead body, and to eat, that's all. Similarly we may go up very high education, but what is our objective, what are we seeing? How to enjoy sense, this body, that's all. And advertisement? "Oh, he has gone with sputnik seven hundred miles up." But what you do? What is your occupation? Sense gratification, that's all. That is animal. So people are not considering how they're implicated with this bodily concept of life.

~ Srila Prabhupada (Lecture, Bhagavad-gita 6.16-24 -- Los Angeles, February 17, 1969)

fact that excess protein is dangerous. The prime danger of excess meat consumption is uric acid (the waste product produced in the process of digesting protein). Uric acid attacks the kidneys and breaks down the kidney cells called nephrons. This condition is called nephritis; the prime cause of it is overburdening the kidneys. More usable protein is found in one tablespoon of tofu or soybeans than the average serving of meat!

Have you ever seen what happens to a piece of meat that stays in the sun for three days? Meat can stay in the warmth of the intestine for at least four to five days until it is digested. It does nothing but wait for passage. Often, it usually stays there for much longer. Medical doctors have found traces of undigested meat remaining in the colon for up to several months. Colonic therapists always see meat passing through people who have been vegetarians for several years, thus indicating that meat remains undigested there for a long time. Occasionally this has been documented in twenty-year vegetarians!

Some vegetarians claim they are more satisfied after they eat. The reason for this is that there are fewer ketones (protein-digestive substances) formed when vegetable protein is digested. For many, ketones cause a trace amount of nausea which one normally interprets as a decreased desire for food due to this uncomfortable and slight degree of queasiness. Although the body calls for more food, the taste buds tolerate less. This is the danger of the popular high-protein diet substances on the market. This abnormally high level of ketones is called ketosis and refers to the state of starvation that the body incurs due to the inability of the appetite to call for nutrition. Most Americans who eat the wrong type of carbohydrates never recognize the high amount of complex carbohydrates required to overthrow this condition. Keep in mind that when the blood ketone level are too high it results in abnormally acidic blood called acidosis.

Meats are frozen for a long period of times. Some meats (especially poultry) are frozen up to two years. Cold temperatures do not kill all species of bacteria. Worse than this, as it is shipped and stored, most frozen meat is thawed and refrozen many times. This is almost unavoidable.

Meat eaters suffer more frequently from various types of food poisoning than vegetarian. Statistics show that every American has had food poisoning at least once. When you've felt ill, had diarrhea or were just a little sick to your stomach, no doubt you had not the slightest idea that you had been poisoned by scavengers living off the dead carcass you just ate.

Meat is costly and it is the most wasteful source of resources. When one removes meat from his or her diet a whole new world of eating opens up. Cooking and preparing vegetarian style is no more time consuming than cooking meat. It costs less than half as much to eat vegetarian as it does to eat meat. There are excellent, nutritious, and easy to prepare vegetarian dishes that are Italian, Chinese, Indian, Mid-Eastern, French, Spanish, etc.

Additionally, one can enjoy many other foods that he or she has never tasted because of the meat craze. Most consumers have eaten no more than five or six varieties of beans and legumes. This is less than 10% of what is available.

Thus there are far more benefits to becoming a vegetarian then there are staying a meat eater. Many meat eaters vow how they were constantly sick, tired, and overweight. But after becoming vegetarian, they are healthy, full of energy and maintaining a perfect weight. They love being vegetarian and it shows. Looks like going vegetarian is the best thing anyone can do for their mind, body and spirit.

References:

A.D. Andrews, Fit Food for Men, (Chicago: American Hygiene Society, 1970)

celestialhealing.net

Milton, Katharine, "A hypothesis to explain the role of meat-eating in human evolution",Evolutionary Anthropology: Issues, News, and Reviews Volume 8, Issue 1, 1999,

"Vegetarians don't eat fish, shellfish or crustacea, but they can still enjoy one of the healthiest diets available.". Vegetarian Society.

Hill, John Lawrence (1996). The case for vegetarianism. Rowman & Littlefield. p. 89. ISBN 0-8476-8138-6.

"Aflatoxins" (1990). Health Protection Branch Issues. Ottawa, Ontario: Health Canada, May. pp. 2–3.Jump up^ "Factory Farming". The Humane Farming Association. October 2010.

Brown, Corrie (2000). Emerging diseases of animals. ASM Press. pp. 116–117. ISBN 1-55581-201-5.

Timm C. Harder and Ortrud Werner, Avian Influenza, Influenza Report 2006, 2006: Chapter two.

28

Food For Vultures

An Appeal To Restaurants

To Donate A Percentage of Their Produce

According to the report called "The Restaurant Revolution", prepared by the International Hotel and Restaurant Association and published in 2000, there are 8.1 millions restaurants in 103 countries with an average of 78,313 restaurants per country.

The low-income countries have approximately one restaurant unit per 618 people; the upper-middle income group has one restaurant unit per 268 people. The average number of outlets across all countries is one restaurant unit per 477 people.

These restaurants have to throw their doors open if the vulture population has to survive. Human beings are presenting a stiff competition to vultures in the matter of food supply. Donating a small percentage of their produce, let's say 2 or 3 percent can go a long way in providing for the vultures. Of course, it has to be raw meat, not cooked meat.

The following is a list of fast food restaurant chains, as distinct from fast casual restaurants, coffeehouses, ice cream parlors, and pizzerias. These brands have a global presence and they should recognize their social responsibility towards preservation of vulture species. These restaurant chains should be persuaded to send meat regularly to vulture restaurants or feeding sites. Vultures have to survive, both the winged ones and wingless ones.

A&W Restaurants
Arby's
Bojangles'
Brioche Dorée
Burger King
Café de Coral
Carl's Jr.
Charley's Grilled Subs
Checkers / Rally's
Chester's International
Chicken Cottage
Chicken Delight
Chicken Licken

Dr. Patel: One friend of mine he told me that this culture is vultures' culture. They eat anything and everything.

Prabhupada: Yes. Not vultures. It is called hog civilization. The hog, they eat anything and they have sex with anyone.

Dr. Patel: Yes, yes. These animals they don't distinguish between their own bodily relatives.

Prabhupada: Nayam deho deha-bhajam nrloke kastan kaman arhate vid-bhujam ye [SB 5.5.1]. This is instruction. Where is culture? Culture is lost. So therefore there is no value of education. And besides that, education means spiritual education. Brahma-vidya.

~ Srila Prabhupada (Morning Walk -- December 19, 1975,

Chipotle Mexican Grill
Chowking
Church's Chicken /
Dairy Queen
Dunkin' Donuts
El Pollo Loco
Fatburger
Five Guys
Hardee's / Red Burrito
Harvey's
Hesburger
In-N-Out Burger
Jack in the Box
Jollibee
Kenny Rogers Roasters
KFC
Krystal
Kyochon
Long John Silver's
Lotteria
Marrybrown
McDonald's
Moe's Southwest Grill

MOS Burger
Nando's
Nathan's Famous
New York Fries
Noble Roman's
Panda Express
Paul
Pollo Tropical
Popeyes Chicken & Biscuits
Quick
Quiznos
Raising Cane's Chicken
Fingers
Red Rooster
Roy Rogers Restaurants
Smoothie King
Subway
Taco Bell
Taco Bueno
Taco Cabana
Taco del Mar
Taco John's
Taco Mayo

> *A vulture may rise very high in the sky -- seven or eight miles -- and it is wonderful to see him fly in this way. He also has powerful eyes, for he can spot a carcass from a great distance. Yet what is the object of all these great qualifications? A dead body, a rotting carcass. His perfection is just to discover a dead piece of meat and eat it. That's all. Similarly, we may have a very high education, but what is our objective? Sense enjoyment, the enjoyment of this material body. We may rise very high with our spaceships, but what is the purpose? Sense gratification, that's all. This means that all the striving and all this high education are merely on the animal platform.*
>
> *~ Srila Prabhupada (Path of Perfection 4: Moderation in Yoga)*

Taco Tico
Taco Time
Tastee-Freez
Tim Hortons
Togo's
Vapiano
Wendy's
Wendy's Supa Sundaes
Whataburger
White Castle
White Spot
Wimpy
Wingstop

Reference:
(http://www.ih-ra.org/publications/)

29

Eating

Civilized And Bestial

by Dvarakadhisa-devi dasi

Consider for a moment the plight of the carnivorous beast. Skulking about the forest brush, sniffing and listening with intense concentration, hunger gnawing at his belly and burning in his eyes, he searches for prey. His meditation is single-pointed in hopes of a kill. But his task is difficult: to find his prey inattentive and unwary. He must be ready -- for whenever the opportunity comes -- and his attack must be swift, fearless, and lethal. And at last it does come -- the kill: the fearful eyes of the victim, the screams of pain and terror, and the stench of fresh blood. For us this would certainly be a repulsive task simply for the business of eating. And this sort of act -- this barbarity, this furtive slaughter -- marks the difference between civilized and bestial existence.

For animals, however, this gross violence is acceptable, without any consideration of right or wrong. The anguish and suffering of hapless prey is hardly the concern of predators in the animal kingdom. And, of course, the killer incurs no sin. For us human beings, however, even to witness such brutal killing is painful, because we are endowed with the quality of compassion. If necessity suddenly forced us to prowl the jungle for creatures to leap on, kill, and devour, most of us would starve. Our bodies, when pitted against the prowess of the animal kingdom, are frail.

Our intelligence facilitates devising other means of nourishment, and our philosophical vision and capacity for empathy lead us to regard the feelings of others.

Nevertheless, our so-called civilized society promotes the slaughter of animals as a necessary element of modern living. We may not have to see the brutality behind those neatly wrapped and ordered packages of red meat displayed under lights in our local supermarkets, but the savage slaughter was there as surely as in the jungle. Although our modern approach to getting food may appear civilized, in essence it is inhuman. Thanks to our superior intelligence, our approach is more sophisticated and controlled,

Where to find eatables, where to find sex, where to find shelter for sleeping, and how to defense -- these circumstances are understood by the animals. There is no need of education. Just like this morning I pointed out. The bird is catching a small fish, "Fut!" He knows where to find out his eatable. And that you cannot do. You also eat fish, but you jump over and take a fish. You cannot do that. But he can do that. He is more expert than you. (guests chuckle) Yes. In the troubled water, he is flying. He can see a small fish and immediately pick it up. Can you do that? So he is more advanced in civilization. (laughter) He knows his techniques. He is greater scientist than you. You cannot do this. A vulture goes seven miles up, and he can see where is a dead body. So even amongst the animals there are many expert scientists than our so-called scientists. But what that science will help? That science may help how to eat, how to sleep, how to have sex. That's all. And that is being done by the animals. It doesn't require any advanced scientific knowledge. Real scientific knowledge is who is God, to know. That is meant for human being, Not this where to find out a fish very expertly. That is being done by a bird. Where is the use of scientists and philosophers? Therefore in the Vedanta-sutra the indication is there that "Now you have got this human form of life. Find out where is God." That is real science. That we have set aside. That we do not touch.

~ Srila Prabhupada (Garden Conversation with Professors -- June 24, 1975, Los Angeles)

and we feel sufficiently removed from the ghastly carnage by the intervention of industry and commerce. Most of us will never see the throngs of cows herded into the slaughterhouse, or hear their pitiful cries, or witness their anguish.

Indeed, what we often see of the meatpacking industry is cartoons of smiling cows, chickens, and pigs dancing across the TV screen, inviting us to relish their tasty flesh. Our language buffers us from any suspicions about the origin of our

"JUST THROW IT ON THE TABLE, AND STEP BACK."

prized sirloin steaks, as we regularly eye slabs of rotting carcasses and refer to them as "cuts of meat," or "tender aged beef." Mothers encourage their little ones to eat their hot dogs, which are stuffed with toxins and intestinal wastes, and smiling waitresses serve hamburger patties comprised of the most repulsive organs of the cow and often containing such substances as earthworms and

> *So different animals in different species of life, they have got one type of consciousness very strong. Just like you can see the vultures. It is a low-graded animal. But it goes four miles above the earth and it can see where is a dead body. You cannot do that. You cannot see even twenty yards after. But the animal, another animal, the vulture, he can see... From four miles away he can find out where there is a dead body. So this consciousness of eating, sleeping, mating and defending, that is common. In one animal or, it is very strong. In another man, animal, it is not so strong. But this consciousness is there. But this God consciousness is not there except in human being.*
>
> ~ *Srila Prabhupada (Srimad-Bhagavatam 1.3.25 -- Los Angeles, September 30, 1972)*

decayed rodents. Yet most of us are somehow convinced that our daily quota of meat is not only safe but necessary for our nutritional well-being, a conviction we maintain even when confronted with the most gruesome details of animal slaughter and meat-eating.

Recent investigations into the practices of a meat-packing plant in the western United States provide a strong challenge to such false security regarding the sanctity of our red-blooded American diet.

Rudolph "Butch" Stanko, owner of the Colorado-based Cattle King Packing Company, is presently facing charges for alleged discrepancies in the cleanliness and purity standards at his plant. The company was a big supplier of meat to the U.S. Defense Department, to fast-food restaurants, and to local supermarkets. Larry Andrews, a former employee, testifies, "He told us not to throw away anything, to use every bit and piece, even the blood clots." The company was accused of regularly bringing in already dead animals and animals known to be diseased to mix in with the ground meat products. In defense against the charges. Cattle King's attorney acknowledged, "Yes, these things happened -- like they do at every other plant in the United States."

Certainly these statements suggest a nasty business full of cheating at the expense of the customer, and you may find yourself viewing your next hamburger with a new wariness. But even without these horrid details, if we think about it objectively, where is the consideration of any real cleanliness or purity when dealing with carcasses? The meat that people are purchasing for their families'

The Vedic culture offers so many nice, delicious foods, and mostly they are made with milk products. But these so-called civilized people -- they do not know. They kill the cows and throw the milk away to the hogs, and they are proud of their civilization -- like jackals and vultures. Actually, this Krsna consciousness movement will transform the uncivilized people and bring the whole world to real civilization.

~ Srila Prabhupada (Journey of Self Discovery 6.5: Slaughterhouse Civilization

dinners is nothing more glorious than contaminated slices of flesh, slashed from animals ruthlessly killed after their brief, miserable, disease-ridden existence, which ended in violence and terror. To ignore the suffering of the animal from whose very body your steak or cutlet has been obtained and to romanticize the business of animal slaughter as healthy, sanitary, and necessary is a kind of madness. What you're getting is simply a package of decaying flesh, toxins, and wastes, and in exchange you implicate yourself in the most horrible kind of violence imaginable.

Human beings possess a higher intelligence and a finer sensitivity that allows for moral judgments. To witness the death of an animal such as a cow, therefore, would be very painful for us. That's our natural human compassion. And yet we eat the flesh of the cow without any qualms of conscience. The heinous act of slaughter may be out of sight and out of mind, but by eating the flesh we become implicated in sin.

According to the strict laws of karma, every human being is responsible for his actions. These actions create reactions, which propel each of us into particular circumstances of happiness or distress. In the case of animal slaughter, a grievously sinful act for one with human discretionary resources, the reaction is that the offender is forced to accept an animal body in his next birth and to suffer the same horrible life and death.

Our meat-eating isn't as bloody as that of the animals hunting in the forest, but in light of our superior capacity for understanding suffering and death, it's far more horrible. We don't need to eat the flesh of animals to survive, and to remove this violence from our lives would create an immediate improvements in consciousness. Being vegetarian may not be the perfection of human life, but it is one of the first steps on the path of perfection.

THE AUTHOR

Dr. Sahadeva dasa (Sanjay Shah) is a monk in vaisnava
tradition. His areas of work include research in Vedic and
contemporary thought, Corporate and educational training,
social work and counselling, travelling, writing books and of
course, practicing spiritual life and spreading awareness about
the same.

He is also an accomplished musician, composer, singer,
instruments player and sound engineer. He has more than a
dozen albums to his credit so far. (SoulMelodies.com) His
varied interests include alternative holistic living, Vedic
studies, social criticism, environment, linguistics, history, art
& crafts, nature studies, web technologies etc.

Many of his books have been acclaimed internationally and
translated in other languages.

By The Same Author

Oil-Final Countdown To A Global Crisis And Its Solutions

End of Modern Civilization And Alternative Future

To Kill Cow Means To End Human Civilization

Cow And Humanity - Made For Each Other

Cows Are Cool - Love 'Em!

Let's Be Friends - A Curious, Calm Cow

Wondrous Glories of Vraja

We Feel Just Like You Do

Tsunami Of Diseases Headed Our Way - Know Your Food Before Time Runs Out

Cow Killing And Beef Export - The Master Plan To Turn India Into A Desert

By 2050

Capitalism Communism And Cowism - A New Economics For The 21st Century

Noble Cow - Munching Grass, Looking Curious And Just Hanging Around

World - Through The Eyes Of Scriptures

To Save Time Is To Lengthen Life

Life Is Nothing But Time - Time Is Life, Life Is Time

An Inch of Time Can Not Be Bought With A Mile of Gold

Lost Time Is Never Found Again

Cow Dung - A Down-To- Earth Solution To Global Warming And Climate

Change

Cow Dung For Food Security And Survival of Human Race

(More information on availability on DrDasa.com)

11422162R00077

Printed in Great Britain
by Amazon.co.uk, Ltd.,
Marston Gate.